The American Drug Cartel

The Whole World Is Delusional

Reality Harmonizer Bob

Written in verse form, this book may use some life experience accounts, and will only use fictional names if needed. "Reality Harmonizer Bob" is cross-cultural, and is not writing an "Autobiography" here, but simply shows a real life neighborly universal approach to the World beyond stereotypes. He also shows that the whole World is delusional about drug cartel issues, and that religious haters of drug cultures based on medicine reasons are also delusional and part of the problem.

Chapter 1 = The Cartel Neighbors & Realities
Chapter 2 = Bible Verses For The Heart, Soul & Mind
Chapter 3 = Better World Keys
Chapter 4 = Things To Pray For Repetitiously
Chapter 5 = Promote 'Spirit & Truth' Awakening Revivals
Chapter 6 = Misconception Non-Conformist Principles
Chapter 7 = 'Spirit & Truth' Awareness Calendar
Chapter 8 = Change For Christ's Kingdom
Chapter 9 = Quotes For Clothing, Accessories & Whatever (1-1114)
Chapter 10 = Healthy Biblical Foods - Nutrition Matters
Chapter 11 = Better World Reprise
Chapter 12 = Better World Poetry
Conclusion and References

CHAPTER 1 = The Cartel Neighbors And Realities

1) We regularly hear about the "Mexican Drug Cartel"; why don't we ever hear about an "American Drug Cartel"?

2) "The American Drug Cartel" is run by political formulas, and is not labeled; frankly, because of the formula - the cartel system is a culture and way of life and is too vast to be particularly labeled as an "Organized Cartel", but this book names various small arm branches of the "Cartel Formula" as basically "American Cartels", because that is what they are whether many of them realize it or not.

3) "The American Drug Cartel" is the largest drug cartel in the World in my

observation, in part because it is the general founder and leader of all cartels worldwide. I say general, because I certainly think it is the leading conspirator via media and politics, and although it may not be the founder of cartels everywhere, it is the conspirator of most growing cartels around the World.

4) "The American Drug Cartel" supposedly does not exist just like Black racism supposedly does not exist.

5) In reality, Black America may have the largest extreme racist population in the World.

6) Black America is not exactly "The American Drug Cartel" = They have a large population who are simply part of the of the political formula and may be representative of having the most risk takers among the crack cocaine connected populations as foot soldiers.

7) The nature of various drugs has something to do with how the top Cartel conspirators plan their game.

8) Drugs have various affects, but are not the main driver; violence, theft, pain, depression, poverty, lost opportunities, and threats are the main drivers of mismanaged drug use and the illegal drug business.

9) The primary conspirators behind "The American Drug Cartel" are Democrat leaders and Democrat media.

10) Democrats push for open borders, and push against Police is formulated in part to support "The American Drug Cartel".

11) Before I go any further - I do not want to demonize the drug culture and cartels. The problem with the drug cultures and cartels is the violence and theft.

12) The fact that there is much violence and theft in various American cartels is a result of demonizing drugs and isolating communities based on that demonizing, and the pressure of going to jail for non-violent crimes actually seems unjust and creates tension that leads to anger and violence.

13) Is it good to have segregated communities that are non-violent from violent communities? Yes, violence and non-violence are apparent legitimate segregation reasons. High theft versus low theft is also another

legitimate good segregation foundation, and God revering versus atheism might be another good reason for segregation, but ethnicity is not a viable reason for segregation.

14) Ideally, the high theft and high violence groups should be detained, rather than having a violent side of free society and a non-violent side of free society.

15) Detainment facilities and their philosophies need much improving beyond the "Old Roman Empire" styles.

16) Why has "One Nation Under God" not highly implemented "under God" into its Prison rehabilitation system yet?

17) What part of "love your neighbor as yourself" tells judges and jurors not to be fair to people? (Leviticus 9:9-18)

18) What part of "Treat others the way you want to be treated" tells judges and jurors not to be fair to people? (Luke 6:31)

19) Leviticus 9:19 in Christ's Bible talks about ways we are to love our neighbors. Verses 9 through 18 in the "King James Version" says, 9 "And when ye reap the harvest of your land, thou shalt not wholly reap the corners of thy field, neither shalt thou gather the gleanings of thy harvest." 10 "And thou shalt not glean thy vineyard, neither shalt thou gather every grape of thy vineyard; thou shalt leave them for the poor and stranger: I am the Lord your God." 11 "Ye shall not steal, neither deal falsely, neither lie one to another." 12 "And ye shall not swear by my name falsely, neither shalt thou profane the name of thy God: I am the Lord." 13 "Thou shalt not defraud they neighbor, neither rob him: the wages of him that is hired shall not abide with thee all night until the morning." 14 "Thou shalt not curse the dear, nor put a stumbling block before the blind, but shalt fear thy God: I am the Lord." 15 "Ye shall do no unrighteousness in judgment: thou shalt not respect the person of the poor, nor honor the person of the mighty: but in righteousness shalt thou judge thy neighbor." 16 Thou shalt not go up and down as a talebearer among thy people: neither shalt thou stand against the blood of thy neighbor; I am the Lord." 17 "Thou shalt not hate thy brother in thine heart; thou shalt in any wise rebuke thy neighbor, and not suffer sin upon him." 18 "Thou shalt no avenge, nor bear any grudge against the children of thy people, but thou shalt love thy neighbor as thyself: I am the Lord."

20) Over punishing is stealing just like any other stealing.

21) The whole World is delusional about medicine and that is part of "The American Drug Cartel" formula.

22) The American Science community has been the World's leading Science community for over a Century in my estimation, and it was dominated by a false racist Science called "Evolution".

23) Godless Science went out of its way to demonize various medicines while glorifying other medicines for the sake of their own pockets and own oppression tactics.

24) Religious communities believed in false Science views in medicine and psychology "hook, line, and sinker".

25) I believe the religious Christian communities falling for corrupt Scientist's views of medicine is the #1 most powerful part of "The American Drug Cartel" formula, because where there is no redemption, there is no hope, and the majority of the Christian religious population bought into the corrupt Science views of medicine, which makes most of Christianity in America the last Century a supporter of heresy instead of true Christianity.

26) Does the fact that most of Christianity supporting heresy in the area of medicine mean that most of Christianity fully supports that heresy? No, it can mean that much of the Christian population was side tracked from the main point of Christianity by the heresy, but did not support the heresy as a way of salvation when approached directly about it in that fashion; howbeit, much of Christianity did not defend people's rights to measured reconciliation as they should according to the American virtue of "may the punishment fit the crime". People have often been over punished and basically robbed of their human rights for being associated with medicinal use, and that is not proper.

27) Do I think the Christian community is the worst player in "The American Drug Cartel"? No, I think they are supposed to be the biggest solution, but have instead helped to be an oppressor and squash hope on the issue. I think the overall majority of Christians have helped to advance the many lies that support violent cartels; such as, "once an addict always an addict", "a person who has used medicine cannot have or control their own money or property", "a person who engages in illegal medicine consumption activity is automatically going to be a thief", and "a person who has engaged in illegal medicine consumption activity should not be paid for labor or gainfully employed".

28) Many religious Christians buy into the lie of Socialist regimes that inhibit private property rights for people who have been consumers of illegal medicines, and that is a trick created by corrupt political Scientist's in favor of slavery and Communist regimes.

29) Legal forms of slavery and Communism generally do not allow for private property rights.

30) Illegal forms of slavery are supported by isolating people from having their own private property rights, which makes many dependent on cartel schemes for a place to rest their feet, and that is not an accidental scheme by many politicians in the past, and advanced corrupt political groups now.

31) "The American Drug Cartel" has been promoted in many ways. First, I will say that the Black communities known for promoting the gangster street dealing lifestyles are not the only promoters, although, they are the most out in the open. Hollywood, and Democrat Political media have been the main promoters of the gangster lifestyle and have used the Black community as a pawn. However, many small cartels monopolized and have been able to clear the chess board with their marketing abilities, and I don't mean an individual natural marketing ability, but the marketing ability of drugs like crack cocaine, which is the biggest and quickest money maker, and I also mean because of the many people attracted to that underground business via being lured or forced in by poverty, or by the money; and the men and women relations that generate around all of that. It attracts many women whether through addiction or money, and that also draws men, whether they are looking to meet someone who appears as lighthearted and friendly, or simply because they may be a victim of the system and meet a potential mate who is also a relatable victim of the systems flaws.

32) It appears that corrupt Scientist's threw crack cocaine formulas into poor Black communities, and Crystal Meth into poor White communities. Was there a plan behind that? Yes, I believe so. There are forms of Crystal Meth (speed) that are not high potency forms and they help White people to work night shifts and make money, and the crack cocaine was created to swindle people's money.

33) Both Crystal and Crack can create poverty, but the higher end Crystal dealers have forms that are less potent. There are very few, if any forms of cocaine that are created to be in a medicinal form, but on the illegal markets there are actually speed forms that are created to be medicinal.

What does that lead me to believe? That leads me to believe that the higher end Conspirator Cartel Scientists are in the Crystal Meth business, and may represent the suppliers of Cocaine also, but they do not even need to be "hands on" as the political class makes ways for them to work independently with the open borders and by having the higher risk takers distract the Police, and that is the BLM leaders and now Antifa.

34) Many people who follow BLM do so, because they believe the lies told to them, but many others, such as some of the Hollywood and successful rich hip-hop artists and NBA players know that they are simply trying to make space for the Drug cartels to work and to usher in a Global government regime. Who knows, maybe some NBA players don't know that, but I suspect that most of them do. It is not as if they do not see all the assault's they support, they willingly and hypocritically do not acknowledge it, likely because they do know the corrupt scheme.

35) When Christianity is wrong on their medicine take, then how is the Drug Cartel a bad business in the first place? Well, the Cartels do not want street medicines legalized. They play games with the marijuana legalizing and delay it, and they push not to legalize medicinal forms of Cocaine, because they are making so much money off it, and are able to run slave schemes, which bring poverty and give them a lot of power and a division between rich and poor. They don't want to lose their business and although, they pretend to hate prison they are hypocritically the biggest supporters of prison as they set up small time dealers, and they are the biggest supporters of killing people who do not pay their debts to the Cartels in a timely fashion while many of those debts are not proper charges, but rather have high interest rates or price gauging.

36) One could debate as to who the biggest illegal drug pushers are - Marijuana or Meth businesses? Marijuana is more highly used and more widely spread and accepted, and it is politically promoted and accepted. That kind of opens the door for other illegal drug forms. Really, the formula's out there just support a lot of independent teams working together it seems.

36) Before I go further in this pyramid analysis - I do not really care to figure out who the biggest pushers are, except to discredit the abusers of people. I think all the laws against proper medicine dealing are corrupt predatory laws made a long time ago, and that the violence and thievery are planned results of politicians opposing legal forms. Am I for people walking around in drunken high's all the time? No, I actually think that there would be less of that if medicines had legal forms and were not pushed on

people by thief markets who live paranoid lives. Pain is a reason to consider taking medicine and the illegal swindling businesses at odds with the general public bring people a tremendous amount of pain, and they know or instinctively know that pain of being robbed, which created rejection or whatever, grows a medicinal demand.

37) I am strongly and confidently opposed to stealing and assault, although, I believe in being fair and merciful in justice to those who are caught stealing, and I believe in keeping the public safe from those who engage in assaults. I am NOT 100% confident of how the legal venues should deal with medicinal issues, but clearly medicinal use is not a crime against human rights and is not one of God's 10 "thou shalt not's" for governing. Using medicine without caution is not wise, is the indication I get from the Bible, and many, carry that to an extreme degree and only view passages that say not to look on strong drink; howbeit, such passages are saying not to crave, or lust after drunkenness, but other Scriptures qualify drunkenness for pain, and lower potency medicine for depression. (Proverbs 31 and Proverbs 23)

38) There are many in religious communities who will say, "how dare you write about drugs and call yourself a Christian!" Well, my answer is that opposing drugs is not what makes a person a Christian, opposing death's permanence by accepting the only Savior who can defeat death is the way to be a Christian and that Savior's name is Jesus Christ (Yeshua).

39) There are many in religious communities who will say, "how dare you write about drugs and call yourself a Christian!" Well, another answer I have for them is that God created medicine NOT corrupt Scientists, and the same supposed Christians opposing me are supporting the corrupt Scientists who refuse to create safer forms of medicine while monopolizing on Hospital injuries from the swindler form's they put into the streets.

40) There are many in religious communities who will say, "how dare you write about drugs and call yourself a Christian!" Well, another answer I have for them is that God created humans equally in His image, and said to "Go ye and tell all people about His saving grace", and how do any people hear from God through Christians without His forgiveness first being transported through Christians to give His fruit of the Spirit a unique accessible relational venue through Christians?

41) There are many in religious communities who will say, "how dare you write about drugs and call yourself a Christian!" Well, another answer I have for them is that God wants honest Scientist's, not crooked ones, and

we should be able to have the freedom to be Scientist's no matter at what level, angle, or experience and we should be able to give our input for the betterment of the community when it comes to creating better safer products for people and in learning and knowing how to advise people to best abstain, or control or recover from various illness, therapies, injuries, and depressions. There is also a debate about whether people should be on long term psychiatric therapies, and I advise that people only take medicine on an "as needed" basis instead of a daily long-term basis if at all possible, and that is good and helpful advice as compared to the popular advice from popular psychiatric long-term remedies.

42) I do believe that if a person commits a theft or assault crime while intoxicated that they should be tried the same as if they committed that crime sober. That is a bigger and more reasonable way of teaching people to use medicine properly or not at all, because it promotes good behavior and responsibility for good behavior instead of blaming everything on medicine, and that is less confusing, and confusion excuses a lot of poor mismanagement of medicines in the high medicine areas run by Cartels.

43) It is likely that the main American Drug Cartel is the smuggling regime. Explanation: You can drive through nearly every City in America and see people on street corners in various areas promoting street drugs, or simply waiting for customers to pass by and wave them in. That is a lot of Cities, and a lot of blocks in each City = That is a huge population of people dependent on drug money, and people who want the products, and / or are lured to use the products more than they prefer. There is a humongous drug smuggling regime in order to supply the drugs to that many venues in every City. Many have called it "The Mexican Drug Cartel", but it is not mostly Mexicans transporting it on this side of the border. It is possible that the Mexican Cartels transport to big stations in America and those larger American Drug Cartel Stations transport to the rest of America, but it is also likely that many risk takers from smaller drug markets simply travel on their own to the big American Stations or to overseas venues or ports themselves and pick up for their own Cities. Probably a mix of both. But the point here is that the smuggling regimes are what represents the Cartels, and the receivers mostly represent what we can call small Cartels, but mostly are just local dealers looking for money and local medicine consumers looking for some relief or an escape from reality or whatever.

44) When I say that the smugglers are the main Cartels, I mean they are the main business hands, but they are not the ones who facilitate it, although many of them may vote to facilitate it. Clearly, the main facilitators are the high-ranking politicians and media persons who have pushed for

open borders, and therefore the main Drug Cartels smugglers are basically working for the Democrat leaders and Democrat media who push for open borders, and they are working together with a global regime in having pushed for open borders in Europe, Germany the UK and other places also. So, the Global regime is working with Drug Cartels to create counter cultures instead of legalizing safer forms of medicine. Many Islamic regimes and LBGTQ activism regimes, and population control extremists all support the Drug Cartel smuggling regime, and the suppression of Police to help continue the Drug Cartels monopoly. That is not a good business when you look at how many people are being killed in Chicago by fighting over small amounts of money because Democrats promote the Cartel business while not allowing their low drug money earners to have savings accounts without going to jail.

45) One must wonder how smaller time illegal drug dealers always seem to be broke? Do Democrats force many small-time drug dealers to filter money to them or are they always broke because of having too many women? I suppose it is a little bit of both for many of them, and there are others who do well and know how to capitalize on it.

46) Frankly, my heart's instinctive view is "how can one be a Christian and not care about the people in drug cultures conspirators or victims"?

47) Who can tell the difference between a victim and a conspirator? Many conspirators were once victims, and many victims were once conspirators.

48) The bigger political formula makes most everyone including active smuggling conspirator's victims, because of the bad predatory laws created from corrupt politics - for the sake of corrupt politics. The true conspirators are the politicians and corrupt media, and even many of them are pressured into being a part of the corrupt political system.

49) OH YEAH, I forgot "The American Drug Cartel" supposedly does not exist - kind of like Black racism supposedly does not exist.

50) OH YEAH, I forgot it is supposedly racist to notice that there are drug promoting groups on street corners in nearly every City in America because many of them are Black, and therefore small Cartels do not exist. Okay, let's get real, they exist in enormous numbers, but I am not pointing that out here to promote prison time for them, unless they are violent assaulters and thieves. I would actually promote minimal tax dodging penalties and penalties for selling drugs without a license to the extent of being in jail until they find a real job and having a good job search network

in the jails. Simply release people when they find a job if there are not thieving or assault charges, or slavery extortion charges, and if there are thieving charges release a person after they pay back their victim's debt while in detainment; that simple – sound's fair doesn't it? It should, and jails should be comfortable setting where peacemaking can be fathomed and taught.

51) Frankly, I don't advocate turning people in for drug dealing under the current system, because it is an unfair system, and it can also be dangerous. If it is someone who is a friend and dealing for the first time and you want to stop them from dealing, I do suggest thinking of creative ways to try and detour them from continuing and it is best for people to figure out to stop dealing on their own rather than to go through the current system. There should be a better system, which I explained about in verse 50 above. Let the routine Policing system handle busting people except in the case where there are violent groups in a neighborhood, well, the neighborhood should not want the violent assaulting types of people running their neighborhoods.

52) PERSPECTIVE BREAK: This book is being written to promote a more neighborly World under God. The perspective is not ignorant to the problems intoxication can bring, but understands that God created medicine's, and society in general has been hypersensitive on the issue of medicine laws, and has created an enormous segregated society, which has qualified a Drug Cartel industry via unrealistic expectations from the drug free supposed drug free side of society.

53) PERSPECTIVE BREAK CONTINUED: The drug free side of society typically loses anyone who is not 100% clean from unpopular drugs from their own drug free philosophy rejecting them due to their philosophy being extreme rather than Biblical.

54) PERSEPCTIVE BREAK CONTINUED: Much and maybe most of the "drug free" side of society is not free from drugs like they think they are, because they use caffeine products. Caffeine is a drug, and many caffeine users who reject other drug users and treat them as outcasts in society do not realize they are as guilty of using drugs as the people they shun for using other drugs. Caffeine users have one of the higher dependency rates over other drugs, in part, because people do not realize they are using a drug. That is one of the formulated tricks of "The American Drug Cartel", which is a trick originating in the Science field.

55) I connect many dots in this book NOT to formulate some kind of big

"Drug War" bust, but to show how we are told a lot of things are wrong that are not wrong, and that the law makers have double standards and hypocritical laws, and unfair justice on the issues.

56) The greater portion of this book connects dots to show that although, I am hopeful that laws will improve - we cannot count on that because the brainwashing is so broad spectrum - therefore, the greater portion of this book will deal with how to improve a neighborly society despite of having bad laws. I will show ways to improve the Drug Cartel half of society also. Frankly, there is one primary way to improve society or keep the peace in society a bit more and that is to oppose stealing and assault whether in drug cultures or in generally drug free cultures.

57) Although, I say we cannot count on laws improving, I am very optimistic that laws can improve, but now is the time to start promoting God's ten commandments universally, which oppose stealing, lying, violent assaults / murder, and polygamy. (Exodus 20)

58) Matthew 5:17-18 shows us that Christ did not come to do away with the law but to fulfill the law.

59) Recognize that God's laws are neighbor loving laws - they are human rights laws, which give us all private property rights.

60) God's laws are advantaging laws to each individual not disadvantaging laws.

61) God's laws give everyone privilege.

62) Frankly, the domino effect of Drug Cartel culture steals privilege from people, but God's laws being promoted among the Drug Cartels despite crooked government and despite some Cartels that are with groups who hate God - Cartels can be given a conscience that respects their employee's property and customers property whether they believe in God as Lord or not. At least more mutual respect can be improved at a much better rate than now and in the past. Nothing in this World will be perfect, but we can create an overall better environment by respecting people's property, because it works mathematically by making the more money hungry Cartels lesser desperate for money because they are not getting robbed as much for example, and that would naturally minimize their "shake downs" on people. (domino effect of good policy)

63) Meanwhile, I promote legalizing 2% forms of all street medicines

including Cocaine. I said ALL street medicines.

64) I suggest legalizing 2% potency forms of all street medicines in pill form by prescription only.

65) Frankly, legalizing 2% potency pill forms may have an effect of minimizing "The American Drug Cartel" demand.

66) Much of "The American Drug Cartel" do not want legal versions taking business away from them, but it actually would work out in their individual success favor, because many people are in the Cartel due to having limited options for being associated with Cartel.

67) How does legalizing safe forms of street medicines soften the bigotry against Drug Cartels? Well, because one main reason aside from money that Drug Cartels have formed is because of bigotry against drug culture that segregates people and makes it difficult to find substantial employment. When medicines have low potency legal forms then the demonizing by some conspirators may continue, but the demonizing will have lesser of an effect and more people will realize that society in general has been hating on people for no good reason. The reason to strongly oppose people, not hate, is for theft and assault NOT for a caffeine or other medicine issue. Howbeit, the opposition to theft should be that of rebuke and expect one to pay back their debt to their victim and then to be redeemed, rather than to be counted out. Assault is another thing. If an assault results in murder - that life cannot be paid back.

68) PRIVILEGE / TRUE AND GOOD PRIVILEGE: "The American Drug Cartel" wants special evil privileges that hold everyone accountable for stealing except themselves. You see today's "Antifa" and "BLM" stealing and doing violence on whomever they please and harassing people and then wanting other people arrested who either defend themselves physically, or respond who respond by opposing one of their murals. TRUE AND GOOD PRIVILEGE is given in God's ten commandments and protects all people from theft and assault. "All lives matter" via private property rights and the right to life is good and proper privilege.

69) "The American Drug Cartel" is not simply an organized group = It is a trained culture. By trained I mean trained in a predatory way. In a way, it does not seem fair to mention Black Americans as part of "The American Drug Cartel", because it is evident that the Democrat Party media tricked and trapped most of the Black population into the Cartel, but the reality is - that is what happened, and they are probably the largest part of it at first as

a slave to the Democrat Party trap, but the reality now is that many high up Black people who have struck it rich via "The American Drug Cartel" pretty much run the Black sector of "The American Drug Cartel" and frankly, have turned various Black populations in America into the seemingly largest foot soldiers for "The American Drug Cartel". Frankly, it is not allowed to be talked about in a reality context like this, but in the context of bragging rights of "being a successful hustler" Black people have regularly post on "YouTube" and "Facebook" and other places about being in Europe and other places around the World and getting their "hustle" on, and those are Americans - spreading "The American Drug Cartel" business around the World and promoting Globalism and supporting Jay-Z and the NBA and drugging up Africa while promoting Abortion and same sex marriage and the whole Democrat Party agenda, which is the real "American Drug Cartel" = The Democrat Politicians and their Media.

70) From my observation, I have never viewed various Black cultures in America as the conspirator, but many of their leaders have grown to join in with the top White Supremacist Democrat conspirators. I suspect there have been Black Muslim conspirators working with the Democrat Party at least since the 1950's, and clearly there were Black slave traders in and from Africa already invested in the Democrat Party since the beginning of American slavery. So, people cannot continue to view all Black Americans as the victim, and we cannot continue to view Black Americans as the victims of racism when many Black Americans are racist themselves and there appears to be larger population of extreme racists in many Black communities than there have been in White communities. Frankly, today's White people are mostly lovers of peace and the Black racist extremists continue to call them racist because they are racist themselves, and want enmity with White people not peace, so they attain enmity by lying about peaceful White people - AS IF "Black lives don't matter" to them". Frankly, the only way they accept a White person as supportive of "BLM" is if a White person will be their slave.

71) There are many major Black conspirators in today's society for the "American Drug Cartels" and for "Global Supremacy". Yes, they have many Black slaves underneath them who are brainwashed, but many of those slaves support their Masters corrupt agenda 100% based on believing the lies of racism and being racist themselves. They have their own racist motivation to support the Cartels and the globalism dictatorship agendas. Now, many of the slaves to the lies who make themselves slaves to a drug culture society who disrespects their own property, which makes them slaves in part, because they believe the lie that "thou shalt not steal" is a White supremacist law - Well, many of them are awakened when

people bring the truth to them that they are the racists. They are taught that "Black people cannot be racist", but when addressed they know they are or can be, but frankly, they have heard for so long that they cannot be, many of them don't recognize they can, but it actually baffles them - many of them have never considered that they could be racist too, and that is part of what makes the racist hatred by some of them so extreme in qualifying their own racist hatred while ignoring character and hating skin tone.

72) I do not have a measure of how deep this goes, BUT another thing that has been wrongly taught to Black American cultures is to settle for rental housing. I assume many ghetto homes are filled with what are called "Slum Lords", who own houses and rent them out. That is okay if they are renting the places out at a fair price. That is okay if the "Slum Lord" is not allowing people to be robbed who may have chemical dependency issues, but I suspect the term "Slum Lord" is a stereotype and originally probably referred to people who rent out houses to people who are into the hustle and partying game while the "Slum Lord" also benefits off their on rental clients being robbed or their clients inviting people in to party and then swindling them. Well, that is part of the Cartel slave culture, and it robs people from ever knowing what it is like to be a home owner. The Ghettos are built up of what are called good "Starter Homes" meaning they are good inexpensive homes for first time home buyers, but the Ghettos have been made unsafe by Cartels who pushed a culture onto Black people that was popularized by Hollywood and Democrat media so as to be an acceptable drug hustling and thieving culture taught that "Stealing is their right" because they were falsely taught that laws against stealing are White racist laws, and they if they are caught and thrown into jail for stealing then that is racism. Okay, so, Ghettos were once a good place for anyone to by a starter home and to be able to save money and buy something later in a more ideal location, but the violence and theft in Ghettos basically ruined that for anyone, and became an area that Drug Cartels mostly only accept people in their who understand or accept the drug culture. Howbeit, I cannot say that anyone is very tolerant of getting robbed; those cultures mostly like to invite outsiders in to rob them; they otherwise, sneak and rob each other and argue as to who stole whatever, and are like the mob - they may severely beat or kill a person they caught robbing them, but it is okay if they who punished that person want to steal when they want to steal so long as it is from someone outside of their little clique. That backfires and many of them still end up habitually robbing from each other especially when not sober, and then there are some groups who have a better handle on the "thou shalt not steal" rules, and this book proposes that the handle on the "thou shalt not steal" rules be promoted everywhere in those

cultures a lot more strongly despite the drug culture intoxication dealing issues.

73) Good privilege is the individual privilege of property rights and rights to life from God's ten commandments.

74) There is a cultural "Slum Lord" connection to government. Look at the LBGTQ activist group as a government activist group instead of as a community of victims. Yes, they served people who at first feared discrimination, but that was never the government groups original purpose. Why is it that LBGTQ activists are the first to know when it is time to go into a Ghetto and start renovating homes for gentrification? I am not saying that "Slum Lords" are all in on this scheme, but the government is aware of "Slum Lords" process in the heart of Drug cartel neighborhoods and when their thieving culture has driven out good neighborhoods for blocks and blocks and the government knows the process and when it is a good time to come in and buy up the place for cheap because there is no competition for it, and they move much of the population there into Government housing and start the process over again elsewhere, promoting their Cartels elsewhere, because much of the money has all been taken from the original areas and people have died off.

75) LBGTQ populations are well known for having an affinity for the Crystal Meth drug, which connects them to Crystal Meth populations. A lot of LBGTQ are all about money. Yes, Black cartel cultures are also all about money, but are always out of money in part due to the nature of the drugs they promote and due to the fact that many of them promote stealing and they get greedy and steal cars and other things from their customers and cause their customers to lose jobs and have no income by doing so, and I guess the next thing they hope they do is to bring them money by stealing for it, and some of them fall for that and just wind up in jail - Black cartels that do that really make no sense at all, but that is what they do - they steal from their customers until they have no means left to be a customer with - maybe they make money off putting people into jail? Or maybe they are just too impulsive to ever figure out that they are screwing themselves - who knows? Maybe they just like getting a little money and showing they are the boss and like bringing pain to people? It is not every Black cartel group who is like that, but there sure have been a lot of those in the past anyway.

76) Well, the LBGTQ groups also have sectors connected to the Cartels. They are far more sophisticated, but there are drug laws so there is still a paranoia that goes along with those groups. LBGTQ is big in Hollywood

and the Supermodel industry and in clothing and designs. LBGTQ has all the high-class street medicine connections and they mainly steer clear of the crack cocaine in the ghettos because they know there is a lot of theft and danger, and they are in fact against the theft and violence; howbeit, people who do strong Crystal Meth tend to be more violent than the crack cultures, because people who do Meth can be awake for days and weeks and actually lose their sanity. But meth is speed and has different forms; there are also forms that help people to work night shift jobs and not act unusual but simply gives people stay awake and physical energy. That is why I say they know of the more sophisticated Scientists, which are probably the same Scientists who sale powder Cocaine to the crack neighborhoods. Black cultures also have powder ties, and today, many White and Black people in drug culture are mixing. It used to be that Crack was dumped on Black populations, but more and more White people are mixed into those populations now, and more Black cartels have moved up into the powder and meth business side of things.

77) So, how do the LBGTQ and Black Drug Cartels connect? Who knows, it is all a big mix, but the LBGTQ opened a lot of doors for international trade when President Obama and the Supreme Court forced "Same Sex Marriage" on all the States. Think about how any terrorist or major Drug Cartel Lord could simply pretend to be gay and marry the same sex just to gain dual citizenship and expand their terror group, Cartel business or Sex trafficking networks.

78) Should Scientists and Global warming Scientists and Global Warming politicians be the only ones to know the formulated drug tricks on society? No.

79) I am sure that certain Democrat Scientists and or Democrat Politicians know more reasons for imposing certain drugs on certain cultures than are even obviously evident.

80) "Hitler's Nazi Troops Took Crystal Meth To Stay Awake." (Huffington Post 3/06/2013)

81) I had heard long ago that Adolph Hitler used methadone on citizens to keep them under his control, but I have not been able to find any current information on that. THE POINT IS that politicians in America who support "The American Drug Cartel" probably promote widespread street marijuana for a reason toward keeping people sedated, and they know what psychological effects it has and even what lies work best on their emotions. They know that crack cocaine steals money and creates

impulsive people in Black ghettos and now in some poor White populations also. They know that certain forms of meth help some of their activist perhaps like "Antifa" to be like soldiers always at work for them, and they know that the LBGTQ populations who do various forms of meth are OCD perfectionists in their work, and that they all facilitate supporting open borders, which helps supply the money chain of Cartels and international gangs that support globalism.

82) Street marijuana is often not as good a drug as people think it is. Maybe it is a good medicine in its medicinal forms, but many people on marijuana in the streets become lesser able to communicate cognitively than other people. You see people who do a lot of marijuana who are talking to themselves and have lost their minds. Street Marijuana can be worse like that some heavier drugs like cocaine, BECAUSE, some street marijuana is laced with other things, which are not marijuana. There is a form of marijuana called "gas", and perhaps some groups put too much of that "gas" in it, but for some reason you see people who simply use marijuana whose minds have become ruined. And then other people who use marijuana do just fine, and still have a sharp mind; howbeit, I have not seen where marijuana users have lesser of a temper than other people - I have actually noticed that marijuana users seem to have more of a temper than other people when they are having marijuana withdrawal. Perhaps I have seen people in a bully culture showing their tempers or perhaps it is the marijuana withdrawals causing the lack of temper control or giving heavy emotions.

83) I mentioned lighter forms of Meth (speed) that help people work night shift jobs and helped Adolph Hitler's army. Well, the stronger forms of meth can be fairly dangerous in that they keep people up for many days. They heighten people's energy and sex drives, but also make people very emotional and violent if people are not highly conscientious about being violent and if they use that form for more than a day. Many people have died from being on meth as long as 2 weeks straight with no sleep. I think that the heavier forms of meth are more dangerous than crack cocaine for one's mental health. Crack cocaine is a swindlers drug and has a quick rush that picks people up and drops them. The good part of that is that they come back to normal sanity pretty quickly, the bad part is that people are tempted to love the rush that quickly helps them to escape their stress or whatever and may want to do too much at once, and they quickly come back down and can tend to be at a lower level of energy than before using and will tend to want more and that costs money and that is why it is known as a swindlers drug and it was created to be that.

84) Crack cocaine attracts swindler and thief dealers, because it is a fast money drug. That doesn't mean that every dealer out there is abusive, but it does attract those types. People can make various forms and the streets today know the various formula's, and some are more interested in knowing the Science of how to make more friendly forms than others. The point here is that some people make forms that really drop people, and other people make forms that don't drop people as much and levels off, which is a more friendly form. I think that the more unfriendly forms use to be more common and today they have a little more friendly forms that don't drop people as much but the drug still has the same nature of a quick rush that goes away, and is there for naturally a swindlers drug.

85) The point of #84 is to show that Scientists new what they were doing when they created the street swindler forms of drugs, and Scientists also have the capability of improving the core drug in the swindler forms into a proper medicinal form.

86) Scientists have the capability of making pain medicines given after surgery lesser addictive, but they don't work toward doing that - instead they try to create new forms of medicines that are less natural.

87) The better medicines are actually the more well-known natural medicines from plants. Some of those medicines like from the "Coca Leaf" have been outlawed via the influence of Scientists who intentionally demonized the medicine in my view. It would be better to take the natural medicine and make it into lesser potent forms, rather than to create more chemically based medicines to experiment with.

88) Making more natural medicines into lesser potent forms would hurt the pockets of the corrupt Science community who gets money from the streets plus from the injuries the street drug cultures cause that put people in the Hospitals. Some of the same Scientists make money off of people going to the Hospital and being prescribed a medicine from the Hospital.

89) Think about how Doctors are very hesitant to give out prescription medicine. There are people who leave the Doctor and cannot get a prescribed pain medicine and then end up getting another type of pain medicine from the streets. Scientists involved in government are well aware of that, and they have lawyers who have scared Doctors away from prescribing medicines. Now, some of that comes natural because of complaints from people who overdosed, but when people overdose that is their own doing. Granted some people can have a lot of pain, get carried away and have an overdose. Therefore, it is possible that the lawyers are

into making money and getting money for a client and that Doctors not prescribing medicines may not be a Drug Cartel Scientist conspiracy, but it does work out in the favor of Cartel Scientists who have a hand in both Cartel medicines + Medical Medicine sales and creations.

90) KEEP IN PERSPECTIVE: When we talk about Drug Cartels = We are simply talking about people who deal medicines; kind of like people who sale beer, Tylenol, or pain medications. The difference is that we have been taught that illegal drugs are the devil, and in a way, it turns out that way, but understand that is because there are 2% proof beers that hardly do anything to make a person intoxicated and there is vodka and stronger drinks. Well, the Drug cartels usually offer the stronger forms, but their products if legalized are not bad in the 2% proof weaker forms.

91) KEEP IN PERSPECTIVE: Even though Drug Cartels sale strong forms of medicine - alcohol dealers also sale strong forms of alcohol, but people can buy those in peace, take them home and mix them to make them weaker and simply buy the stronger forms to get more for their dollar while making them last longer because they do not need much of the stronger forms = they just dilute and mix a little at a time or make many weakened mixed drinks to serve to a whole party with one small strong drink bottle being diluted. In Drug Cartel environments where people are not swindling and hustling consumers - those consumers can dilute and weaken the street forms with marijuana or something else also, and when they do that - it is not so bad and does not bring out a devil in people, BUT in many or most settings in the Drug Cartel neighborhood hustles people are rushed, robbed and even ambushed or threatened to be ambushed and don't use medicines without being rushed and they end up rushing them down and being paranoid all for the purpose of a greedy cartel who wants to swindle more money out of them and then throw them out on the street in hopes they will be desperate and find ways to beg, borrow or steal more money, and if they don't do that for them - then they usually just let them walk, but basically stole part of the same product from them that they sold them, and emptied their pocket while they were briefly intoxicated. That happens with the stronger drugs mostly, but can also happen with marijuana when a person does not know what is going on or cannot react fast enough. A person on marijuana can be pick pocketed and not know it or could even be "date raped". SO, the fact that people use the stronger intoxicants to rush them and steal their money does not make the drug as bad as it seems to the general public. People often do not spend all their money on a drug like people think - they actually are often robbed or overly charged in some cases.

92) Technically, in a weakened medicinal form - the street medicines are basically various depression, pain and anxiety medications, but Cartels and Politicians want them demonized so as not to legalize safer forms, because they make a ton more money from swindler groups running the drug sales business over Health organizations doing it.

93) WHY ARE POINTS #90-92 IMPORTANT? Because, there is a thing called "Drug Rehab", and today's drug rehabilitation has also been set up to help "The American Drug Cartel" formula.

94) PREFACE: "The American Drug Cartel" and the Democrats psychological war agenda coincide. The Democrat politicians their media, Hollywood, and their music venues psychological war and lies are what run the Cartels.

95) "The Mexican Drug Cartel" in my view is basically a slave or supplier for "The American Drug Cartel" scheme, which is set up by Democrat politicians, their media, and Hollywood who have created an entire culture, which includes about 50% of Americans in my estimation, which is about 150 million Americans who are directly affected by the Cartel schemes. Some of "The Mexican Drug Cartel" may disagree with me, and want to claim that they are the boss. Well, in a sense they are the boss on their end; it is possible they boss the Democrat Americans around some, but basically, what I am saying is that America provides their large consumer demand and "The Mexican Cartel" is a big supplier to the main ports in the USA, but it is likely USA ports who disperse out throughout the USA for the most part. "The Mexican Drug Cartel" may supply elsewhere in the World also, "The Mexican Drug Cartel" has not been highly observed by me - I live in America, and I have studied "The American Drug Cartel" a lot not "The Mexican Drug Cartel".

96) In my view "The Mexican Drug Cartel" is simply a branch of "The American Drug Cartel", BUT "The Mexican Drug Cartel" has more access to the farm sources for the drugs. Clearly, much of the Heroin comes to "The Mexican Drug Cartel" from Afghanistan and that is how there is a globalism connection that interests Democrats via Islamic nations and Mexico, although, I don't think Mexico is highly interested in globalism "The Mexican Drug Cartel" has some interest in globalism due to the drug trade.

97) When you piece all this together you realize that it is actually realistic when libertarians talk about how legalizing can get rid of the violence, because in reality all the Drug Cartels do at the core is sale medicine, just

like a liquor store sales beer, and there is not fighting or violence in the liquor business because there is not paranoia and sneaking and worrying about going to jail for it. The violence basically comes from fear of going to jail, and then people being paranoid that another person may accidentally or purposely get them caught. People become use to being bullies when threatening people to be careful; some people handle the pressure fine and don't get violent and others let the pressure make them into a major bully and they wind up putting everyone else at risk to be their fall guy while only protecting themselves.

98) Because of the paranoia and thieving domino effect in Drug Cartel cultures - many people are used like servants and slaves, because they have nowhere else to go, and they end up being risk takers and errand boys for the people who let them have a place to lay their head. That lifestyle creates a monopoly for the people at the top of the pyramid, and greed simply grows, which is another reason for much violence and continuing to make thieving acceptable so long as it feeds the leaders of big and small groups in their system. But not everyone loves the violence because clearly, people want to see a better day tomorrow. Therefore, there is hope in teaching people to revere God's ten commandments in Cartels despite shortsighted laws of man.

99) THE WHOLE WORLD IS DELUDED: People think coffee is healthy while picking on other supposed drug addicts. Caffeine users think nicotine users are losers; that is hilarious in a way, isn't it?

100) THE WHOLE WORLD IS DELUDED: Religious people in America treat drug use as the unpardonable sin, but the same people doing that use caffeine products more regularly than illegal drug users use illegal drugs.

101) THE WHOLE WORLD IS DELUDED: People go to drug rehabs to be told that once they are an addict that they are always an addict and cannot help it, and they use that to try and imprison them and get government funding while having them count their clean and sober days all while having free coffee at every meeting.

102) It takes 3 or so days to clear oneself from the addictive withdrawal phase of caffeine just like with any other drug / medicine.

103) Caffeine has one of the more difficult withdrawal phases because of headaches and memory issues as the main withdrawal symptoms.

104) There is a lot to know and understand if you want to improve society by improving the Drug Cartels and I think we are going to have to improve the Drug Cartels because that can happen a lot more quickly than government improving. Many people think that thinking in terms of preaching gospel and ten commandments to Drug Cartels and educating Drug Cartel cultures about drugs and nutrition is not the proper way to go, because they are outside the law, and we are supposed to respect "Caesar's Laws". WELL, it is Caesar or his wife who has created the double standard, which supports the Drug Cartel industry and promotes their business = they basically have hypocritical laws, but I am not proposing that we promote drug use or sales - I am simply saying that we should teach people what the proper and more safe ways of living are in a real way. Teach them nutrition, teach them about how they are being cheated and swindled, and teach the dealers that it is wrong to swindle, advocate the legalizing of safer low potency medicinal forms, strongly oppose and forbid killing, assault, and stealing whether in or out of drug cultures, and teach real Sciences and psychology of rehabilitation such as, the withdrawal phase only being 3 days, and that using after that is a choice and not an addiction. Take the Bible stance in stating that the careless use of medicine is not wise, but it does not say that it is the unpardonable sin to use unwisely, nor does it say that wise use is a sin at all.

105) "The American Drug Cartel" is not designed to be a lot of conspirators - most of the stronger drugs were thrown into poor Black communities while media exaggerated about racism in order to keep them segregated so as to impose Drug Cartels on them. Now, that is an easy pattern to see - you can call it an assumption or theory, but it is clearly what happened and still happens today with Democrat media falsely accusing racism to anger Black people, but today, many Black racist groups have joined in on the White Democrat media scheme as partners in promoting segregation, for the sake of Communism, for the sake of segregation helping the more organized Drug Cartels, and for the sake of globalism, which some people like because they think it brings more Drug Cartel revenue. Why would they want a more violent version of Drug Cartels to grow globally when they themselves have a higher percentage chance of being killed? It is hard to say, but perhaps they think that all drugs will become legal in that environment, and that they will be able to usher in a military Police who put a chip inside of all citizens. If that is what some think - it will not be as pleasant as they envision. I suspect that leaders and media have that plan but many followers are influenced by Drug Cartel culture, which is a huge population and they are tired of our predatory drug laws, and losing various freedoms due to drug charges, and that is one thing I cannot say they are

wrong about = People should not lose freedom's for medicinal consumption - they should be able to go to a rehab class that does not interfere with their jobs in most cases, and they should be advised to own their own private property so they are not kicked out of an apartment for being caught drunk or using a medicine one time. Some rules are understandable, but without mercy they just create homelessness and exasperate the problem that grows a market for predatory dealers on the consistent or growing homeless population. Better yet, legalize the 2% low potency pill forms by prescription only and you solve a lot of problems.

106) To show how strong the divide is and one thing that feeds the communication divide, which blocks the messages of God's human rights commands - Much of the Christian community claims that when a person who once did drugs is drug free is now saved, and being drug free shows that they are truly saved. That is not salvation = That is heresy. That is basically indicating that relapse or any drug use is the unpardonable sin and that stopping it is salvation, which eludes that any association with drugs or people who are affected by drugs is forbidden. So, how is the Christianity of "love your neighbor as yourself" advanced under a message like that?

107) It is certainly a good message to abstain and separate yourself from where drugs are prevalent because that is a healthy lifestyle and there is a lot of hustling and pressure around drug culture society with man-made laws being the way they are today in supporting swindler forms of drugs instead of safe legal forms that are NOT marketed by swindlers that people run into when they leave their home to go almost anywhere in a lot of high drug areas. BUT people surrounded by the drug cultures often cannot help where they are, because the housing in those areas is what they can afford. Also, it is not the unpardonable sin, and people who live in heavy drug areas deserve to be protected by God's ten commandments, which give us private property rights just like anyone else does, and that includes the drug pushers, the drug consumers and the neighbors that live close by them and have nothing to do with it. God's neighbor loving messages are just as good for all of them as for anyone else, and frankly, God's neighbor loving messages are not spoken on enough in the drug free zones either, there is a little too much of a "be perfect or else" type messaging going on and that will never happen, and that message does nothing to help areas where the Democrat politician formula places Cartels and qualify stealing and assault. It does not take a whole lot of teaching for people to realize that not treating other people fairly and with dignity is wrong and whether people believe in God or not - good teaching helps to give them some good conscience and to recognize some benefits of more peace and better

dealings, and that is capable of a good domino effect instead of a bad one.

108) Obviously, Crystal meth has been around longer than I am aware of, and did not simply begin in America or Mexico, or perhaps it did come from Mexico back when Hitler was using it - I doubt it. So, the part of my theory about the American Cartels spreading drugs all around the World is debatable as to what percentage the USA promotes drug culture around the World. It is evident that drugs are so prevalent in the USA that if Mexico is the primary supplier of drugs to the USA and USA ports disperse drugs in the USA - that many people for a long time have been capable of international travel in the USA to other Countries, and probably do some small time smuggling into other Countries, but the point here is that regardless of how often or to what degree that may happen - Our media has promoted drug cultures via Hip Hop music and movies Worldwide and it seems especially in Africa, Europe, UK, Arab Nations, and seemingly also in China. Despite those nations having their own illegal drug issues - many of the "street hustle cultures" I have seen in recent years on video in those Nations resembles the USA where rap music became big and was used as a catalyst to promote the Drug Cartel culture and to basically make it look sexy.

109) After acknowledging that America's Cartel lead around the World is mostly ideological and psychological warfare run affecting many nations and creating followers who buy into their politics of partial Anarchy, but really a masked Anarchy while ushering in a Dictator supremacy regime - I will point out that China has been a fairly big supplier of illegal drugs to America. A very strong dangerous drug called "Flakka" comes from China and was known for making it into parts of Florida at a higher rate than other places in America. That drug was so strong that I suspect it was easy to track by ICE agents as people would use the drug and then be rolling around in public streets.

110) Clearly, various drug forms have to come from the Science communities, and some of the corrupt sides of the Science communities in reality are Evolutionists and Climate Change Scientists and they are both probably representative mostly of the Evolutionist community and corrupt Politicians. Clearly the corrupt politicians in the Democrat Party and some who have been chased out of the Republican Party in America have supported open borders - do you wonder why anymore after reading the first 109 verses of this book?

111) The drug laws in America have been corrupted and predatory for

years and years, and the average American did not realize it because clearly people are weary of others being intoxicated and the dangers of being overly intoxicated on anything. The corruption started with Scientists and politicians and power-hungry mafias or Drug Cartels who wanted to manipulate the system in their favor, but I would have to go with Scientists and Corrupt politicians being the biggest players, because Drug Cartels usually just like the Cartel culture or benefits, but the Drug Cartels who become super rich typically get more involved in Politics later on after having been steadily at the top of their game. Some Cartels got into the game because they recognized the corruptness of the double standard laws in medicine, or saw a growing demand that was not manageable under the current laws. Do I think a person should give into that lifestyle? No, but everyone cannot see it as I do, because they may have grown up more manipulated by the system than I have been, and may have had easy open doors to it, so, in cases like that - I cannot say who is making a bigger mistake - I can say that a person who is not loving their neighbor as themselves under God is the one making the biggest mistake whether in a compromising situation or in a good straight forward set of circumstances.

112) There is a lot of natural psychological warfare not just planned. The planned psychological warfare is all the Democrat media lies used to anger Black American, and not just to anger them but mostly to intimidate them at first but over the years the anger grew and grows, and many of them have caught on to the game now that we have social media. But most Social media is Democrat run and they block the messages regularly that expose the Democrat scheme.

113) So, "The American Drug Cartel" is actually the Democrats using "The Mexican Drug Cartel" as a pawn and for the most part they dumped all the burdens on our Nations Black communities, which they had segregated and by doing so were able to conceal many of the drug issues that plagued the communities for many years. Those drug issues were imposed not inbred, but over time the Black communities have continued to have successful people come out of them, and those caught up in the Cartel games imposed on them have learned to play the game in their favor, but the lies are so many that the messages of true justice have continued being perverted by Democrat media. Howbeit, both the true messages of justice and the Democrats unjust mob rule messages are both being heard more than ever today, but unfortunately, the Democrat Party is the super-rich media party and get the negative messages out there more than the positive messages are hear; howbeit, the truth is consistent and easy to recognize in a world full of lies, but many people have fallen in love with revenge messages based on false statistics and false accusations, while

probably most people have fallen in love with the money they can make off of playing games with the messages which promote the Anarchist Drug Cartel hustle game. I am not saying, which one will be predominate - I am just saying that both good and bad messages exist and the good messages are available more than ever now also, and there really is a good chance for a revival of sorts that brings a greater level of peace for a long time, and that is the side to always hope for no matter how predominate the negative side of things is; but frankly, there is much to be hopeful for right now, because both the positive and negative side of things are large, but usually the negative side of things is larger than the positive, and now it is more even than ever and the positive side of things has won many time when they have been outnumbered, because their mission is more centralized and serious, whereas, a lot of manipulators exist on the negative side who won't stand up when they see opposition that has been patient rise up and show they are bigger than them.

114) Think about the fact that when Hollywood and Democrat owned media started promoting gangster rap, which promoted Drug Cartel gangs in Black communities; well, the media already knew that existed. That started coming around even before cable. America only had about 3 to 5 channels before that time, and the media did not simply want to promote that lifestyle because of talented people and because they thought it was unique = They wanted to promoted it because it was a business that they were already familiar with and it was a business that they helped create through their Evolutionist's and via being able to conceal via segregation. Think about it. Think about Republicans lifestyles = Go to work, go home, go to Church, maybe go hunting, and hardly talk to anyone except the wife or friends of the wife and husband or the husband's or wife's extended family; and most Republicans generally viewed that lifestyle as a clean, safe and neighborly lifestyle while letting everyone else also have their space and freedom and as they call it simply, "staying out of trouble". Republicans in the 1960's an 1970's and even the 1980's were basically clueless as to what Hollywood and other party goers had going on in our Nations ghettos as they would dump drugs in the hoods and help to create a supply for their Hollywood parties and a diversion from Hollywood while likely letting many Black Americans take the fall and go to jail if caught; not that they would set them up, although some might, but simply that they let them take the risks for a few dollars. They ended up creating a cheaper version of the drugs that had a higher demand because although, they made cheaper drugs the drugs they designed for Ghettos had a quick rush and a quick drop, which would make a person crave another quick rush in hoping to extend the euphoria. That later became an epidemic in part because people were fighting over money and drugs and there was a lot of

violence here and there, and that created some fear and drugs also became a medicine used to help cope with the fear and to help nightwalkers to overcome their fears of walking the streets at night. Prisons sentences were extended under President Reagan for the quick rush crack cocaine in the 1980's because there were too many shootings by the crack dealing cartels. There was no racism reason for the longer sentencing - the reason for it was to cut down all the killing that came specifically from those gangs. The same type of killing from crack dealing cartels still happens some today, but most reasonable cartel groups have learned how to deal more calmly; howbeit, some have not learned and new independent dealing groups sometimes arise and don't know the History of the violence and decide to be greedy and violent, although, there are enough other groups more familiar to speak to their conscience now, so, although there are more violent groups periodically the violence is not nearly as often as it was in the 1980's when crack cocaine first hit the streets.

115) Understand when I say that Democrat media promoted gangster rap - they told rappers who talked about the gang life in their raps that they would be able to strike it rich if they rap for them, because Democrat media knew it owned the media platform and had the ability to draw an audience for anyone they wanted to. I am not saying that the rappers aren't talented, but I am saying that they could have said the same thing to a Black Christian rapper and made them famous if they had wanted to, but I am saying that the Democrat media wanted to make gang life a culture and make it more popular in Black communities rather than a dread due to the violence; instead they brought in many attractive women into the music and videos and made it all look like a fun thing, and there is some fun to the games but it is mostly a business NOT fun.

116) Democrat media already knew how the cartel businesses were run in the ghettos before rap and movies of the culture were introduced. Democrat media already knew that they had neighborhood gangs battling over money, and that the money could be good at times, but that they were not allowed to have savings accounts and therefore had no good place to keep their money. Media already knew that although money was good - it usually couldn't last unless someone was really clever, but not only clever but had other clever people to depend on who knew all the loopholes in the business system rules. Media already knew that only a few people could make it big and that everyone else just had to figure it out as they go and that a large number of people would fall flat on their face or land in jail when they promoted the lifestyle. Later on, the communities learned how to manage and settle with being more conservative and simply surviving

and it is true that once a person gets a reputation it could be hard to move out of the Anarchy system created by the Democrat leader and into the true free market system. It is not as difficult today, but there is more of a psychological battle and a lot of oppressors who simply don't like to see others succeed, and frankly many of those oppressors are people who just feel stuck in the lower part of the system due to not conquering an addiction and they like to declare that other addicts cannot conquer it either - claiming it is impossible and demanding they don't even try, because they really want to insist that people they have found "dirt" on so to speak be stuck being their co-dependent partying partner is usually the case, but other oppressors are typically people unfamiliar with the drug culture who simply stereotype all people involved and just simply like to predict that nobody scarred by that culture will succeed unless they prove otherwise and they will "kick them while they are down" basically, and it sometimes does knock a person down who is trying to get up, but that type of person usually keeps trying to get up and is usually able to stay up at some point barring they don't die or get a jail sentence or something during a fall first.

117) HERE IS ANOTHER PROBLEM WITH HOW DEMOCRATS IMPOSED CARTEL LIFE ON BLACK COMMUNITIES BACK IN THE DAY = Democrats not only influenced segregation, but they created more segregation when they threw drugs into Black communities. They also threw abortion clinics into Black communities not just to kill Black babies but because they wanted to throw pimp games into Black communities and make abortion convenient for Pimps. The main point here is that when they tossed drugs into Black communities back in the 1970's and 1980's at its worst and some before that also; they had people place drugs to sale in young people's hands and they put them in debt eluding they had to come back with a certain amount of money from what was placed in their hands. Well, there was a close watch on taxable dollars as always. SO, HERE WAS THE PROBLEM = the Democrat Cartel scheme had young Black people trapped in having to deal drugs to pay off debts to the suppliers who dumped it on them, which took their time away from gainful employment and was a lot of stress. Without gainful employment any money they made was practically worthless except for a weekend thrill, because if they bought a car or house then the government would come and say, "how did you get that car or house when you don't have a job?" So, not only could they not have a savings account but they could not buy property, and their time and peace were taken from the pressure; therefore, they would adapt and learn to like other things such as some weekend fun, or having "partners that understood them and would work with them". It was not an attractive venue back then in the same way it can

be nowadays. Even today, it has its hardships, but it became so rampant that it is natural and apparent that people found ways to survive and do things without over doing it, and many understood how people got trapped in it and were understanding and supportive of each other basically staying out of trouble and people minded their own business and many were not hated for staying out of the game due to knowing the risks are not ideal. Society in general knows today and for quite some time knows that the legislation is out of kilter and not exactly fair and that the business had been promoted by our own media while having a double standard. Society in general knows that the greater problem is assaults and stealing, and are not highly opposed to drug dealing groups except for the violent one's. However, a large part of society thinks that drugs simply create the violence and that is a misconception except sometimes when a person is intoxicated, but it is the paranoia and lack of rules and lack of price gauging accountability that can create some greed and violence also because dealing groups and consumers are not protected from assault and theft except for setting up their own protection among themselves.

118) Another problem with #117 is that Democrats also are responsible for much of the corrupt Prison legislation and hypocritically pretend they are not. The Democrats created many things in Prison that I can no longer keep up with unless I do major research on it, but they found ways to make money off of the Cartels paying people's way in and out of jail, which continued to encourage Prison instead of contesting Prison sentencing for non-violent drug crimes. The rightful system should have the punishment fit the crime - in other words if someone is caught stealing 100 dollars then really - they should serve time in detainment while being able to work while in detainment to pay back the 100 dollars they stole and is should be at the discretion of the victim is 100 dollars is enough or if they should pay up to 7 times that amount at the maximum and then when it is paid off if they show to be repentant and have been a peacemaker while in detainment and they have a job waiting for them outside of jail - then it should be fine and a good thing to go ahead and release them and consider them reconciled and redeemed. A payout system pays the system, the political system, the courts, but not the victim. If a person steals a car, then it takes longer to pay that off, but in some cases full coverage insurance pays for a stolen car instead of the offender, and the offender either sits in jail too long or may even have a payout option, which may let them out as an unrepentant thief. Repentant thieves are not a problem it is the unrepentant people that are not neighborly who pose problems. There is the question of who is a repeat offender and who will not be, but that can often be figured out based on one's behavior or on the nature of the offense, but everything cannot be based on guessing who is truly

repentant versus faking repentance but the system should support a person paying back their debt to a victim and showing repentance and basically let them go after that is seen, and the detainment facilities should always have a philosophy of being a place of peacemaking and accommodating that atmosphere rather than the traditional "Old Roman Empire" style, which was not a Christian nation based form of Prison.

119) The problem with what Democrats are doing today - is they are pretending to be against Prison while siding with unrepentant criminals instead of repentant one's because Democrats have not been able to succeed in supporting oppressors at the level they had wanted to. Think about it - Democrat leaders and Democrat media is not hiding anymore = They are not arguing to legalize drugs anymore - when they did argue to legalize drugs they were playing a game and delayed legalizing proper forms of marijuana for years and years by debating, which forms should be legal - it would have been easy to simply settle on one low potency pill form first and start with that, but they were being hypocritical about it and loved the money they made from the Cartels in the streets plus the money they made off the prisons for arresting non-violent offenders. The real issue is that the Justice systems top concentration should be on protecting people from assault and from theft, and when they concentrate on that more than on drug games, then people get the message and are more afraid to commit an assault or theft because they know that is high priority and then they also understand in their conscience that people are valued and that other people's safety is a high priority of enforcement and it gives people full circle a little more respect for people's lives and personal property, also because a potential thief's property is also more protected and some people become thief's after their property had been disrespected; so, focusing on enforcing against assault and theft if highly beneficial over focusing on drugs and other things as much.

120) So, who is the real bad guy? Who is the one we should all go after that is causing all the problems? Well, we are all bad, and the key is to use God's governing tactics, which key in on "love your neighbor as yourself" laws and human rights to life and rights to private property laws. The people who do clear breaks of those laws against another person are the ones who need to have enforced reconciliation reasonably and fairly.

121) KEY POINT: The Drug Cartels can be directed in a good direction, but Democrat leaders and their media want to direct them in a barbaric direction.

122) KEY POINT EXPLAINED: What is the bottom line of what Drug

Cartels do? They sale medicine without parameters in an Anarchist business form. Most of the medicines that the poorer populations receive are the stronger swindler forms of medicines, because lower class groups are their own bosses and oftentimes are simply groups of swindlers. The richer groups sometimes have a larger variety of medicine options including more medicinal low potency options, or they have more pure options with longer lasting affects although, they may be strong for pleasure reasons instead of being used rightly for therapy. There is no regulation so, rich people can also be dealing with swindler groups, but also have knowledge of higher up the ladder dealing groups because those groups have a way of making themselves known to the wealthy.

123) WHAT IS THE "GOOD DIRECTION" IN THE "KEY POINT"? Drug Cartels naturally formed from crooked or misled Scientists (likely crooked) who declared some good medicine as bad medicine and outlawed it while only primarily making strong forms of those medicines for street dealers to deal for them without regulation. Think about a crooked Scientist group wanting to make a lot more money off medicines that cannot be regularly prescribed in their strong forms, and influencing legislators to outlaw the medicinal form altogether while placing stronger swindler forms into the streets. It was likely more than one person, because the main producers of the drug would have had an interest and a crooked politician or crooked political group may have had more interest in a scheme than a pure Science group, but political people can know Science pretty well also. KEY POINT: The good direction would be to have the Cartels acknowledge that they know there are safer forms of their medicines either available or capable of being produced and legalize the safe medicinal forms into a 2% potency pill form available by prescription only; and doing that will open the eyes of people to understand that we are simply talking about strong medicines versus diluted and controlled medicines, and that the biggest problem with medicines is when they are being used for the purpose of swindling. It is not ideal for any person to use a strong medicine except to buy it strong to save money and to dilute it if it is deemed as needed.

124) WHAT IS THE "BAD DIRECTION" IN THE "KEY POINT"? Democrats can let the Drug Cartels take over in their Anarchist form and continue letting swindler groups be the primary drug runners and give them even more power while the lies about medicine continue on and the drugs are pushed on even more people and used to place more people in poverty and the Democrats crash our system and run their Drug Cartel games on all the people who Democrats invite across our borders while Democrats usher in a Military Police system and use Cartels to majorly sedate and control the entire population, and they won't know what hit them, because

they will trust what the Police allow them to have from the Cartels just like they trust that Coffee is good for them. This might not become common practice, but it could potentially be one of their (Democrat leaders) optional plans of how to take over for Globalism. Of course, their plans may be far more barbaric than that, and as a matter of fact - they are, because some of that barbarianism with Antifa is already happening, but they would like to increase that barbarianism to a point where they would insert the Military Police system that I mentioned and the Cartel takeover plans would follow behind that after the barbarianism potentially would bring more mass poverty.

125) The "key point" in short = the good direction qualifies medicine as medicine and stops playing the corrupt Science game of acting like some medicines are the devil when the truth is that any medicine can cause illusions in its strongest form and any medicine can serve a more medicinal purpose in its weakest forms. There are exceptions in times of intense pain where stronger medicine is helpful toward created a better situation than screaming and wrestling in pain would be without strong medicine.

126) The "key point" in short = the good direction qualifies low potency medicinal options of street medicines in regulated prescription form.

127) The "key point" in short = the good direction ends up negotiating with Drug Cartels toward ending a "drug war", then taking a "law and order" approach.

128) The "key point" in short = the good direction may help us to discover better options with the stronger forms of medicines, because frankly, the Cartels may not come to an agreement of stopping their business altogether. That is where it gets a little complicated, because would low potency legal forms be purchased from the same illegal cartel farm base? It may be difficult for the government to rationalize doing business like that with a former Anarchist group, but I think some steps to take will naturally be revealed.

129) The "key point" in short = the good direction acknowledges that assault and theft need to be opposed whether the Cartels or active in business or not, and assault and theft needs to equally be opposed for Cartel customers or conspirators as equally as for anyone else.

130) The "key point" in short = the good direction acknowledges that IF there is a "drug war" instead of simply taking the "law and order" approach; then that "drug war" is supposed to be against the biggest moving pieces

and the main farms, not against medicinal consumers and small-time dealers, and maybe not even against port receivers, but primarily against the main base suppliers.

131) If the "drug war" were real and proper it would not be against all the receivers while not going after the core suppliers. If there was a real "drug war" it would seem easy to go after the main suppliers, because they have to have big bases to put out the level of drugs they put out. When you look at the big picture like that you have to wonder if there has ever been a real "drug war" or if it is all just words to continue locking people up for petty consumption and small deals for the sake of justice system and prison bail money, and other ways for politicians and government to get money such as government funded rehabs, and government funded halfway houses as well as addiction houses funded by government and rehab programs in homeless shelters that prevent people from working but get funded by the government based on the "drug war", which claims that "addicts cannot work a job and have money for 6 months" and other bogus claims, and therefore the government needs to help pay for their housing in rehab facilities. That is bogus in a way if you think about it, because one "relapse" puts people back in some of those 6-month programs not allowed to work. Now, the only valid part is that a person can lose all their money to thieving cartels in just one relapse, and that does leave people stranded, but the solution for that is to tough it out at work until you catch up on your sleep and then keep working after you caught up some on sleep and then get paid again and learn not to lose all your money in a way that leaves you stranded; that is called having a second chance with their money and learning how to manage their own money without being shamed into thinking they cannot make their own decisions and not letting the system support rationalizing letting other people boss them around about their money. Let people know that their money is their money and they need to learn to make it work for their most basic needs no matter whether they budget it all perfect the first few times or not - people need to learn how holding onto their own money can help them get from point A to point B instead of always being declared ineligible of private property rights, which includes that your money is your own private property = "thou shalt not steal", and "thou shalt not covet", which also means don't tell people how to spend their money for your own gratification - they spend their money to take care of their own needs first.

132) Did "The American Drug Cartel" develop completely by conspiracy or did many complimentary parts happen one thing at a time by chance? Well, we live in a new era of the World that the Bible refers to as "pharmacia", which I will just call the "Pharmacy Age". (Galatians 5:19-20;

Revelation 9:21; 18,23; 21:8, and 22:15) The fact that we live in a big new medicine invention age, which began before 1900 leads me to think that the Drug Cartel results may not have been planned; howbeit, it is possible, because the more natural medicines were discovered in the early 1900's, and the perverting of demonizing medicine happened fairly early in the 1900's, and they were outlawed and ever since Scientist's have been working to create various chemical forms of medicine rather than using the most natural remedies, and ever since there has been various mafia's who dealt some of the more natural drugs in an underground system that grew. Therefore, it is possible that at some point various political interest groups conspired various cartels in poor neighborhoods that later graduated to finding Black communities as easy prey due to segregation. Was it a racist plan at first or was it merely convenient money? It was surely a mixture of both, and I don't know whether the easy money had more influence or the race issue had more influence at some point. My guess would be that it was really more about the convenience and money to dump things on the Black communities and simply be able to say, "it was the Black guy that did it", which may have been true, but the White guy dumped it on the Black guy to start with. Certainly, there were Democrats who jumped at the notion to oppress Black people soon after they saw the results, because Democrats were the Party of KKK and Jim Crowe at the time, and KKK is an Evolutionist group and today and all throughout the 1980's when crack cocaine was invented - the Democrats have continued being the Party of racist Evolution, which I remind you is a false and corrupt Science given the power to influence legislators and make predatory drug laws.

133) I NEED TO BRING THIS OBVIOUS POINT OUT INTO THE OPEN: Although, many Black Americans are very racist hateful toward me for being White today, I still must point out that what happened to Black communities with the "Drug Cartels" was NOT their doing - it was dumped on them for certain, and they were certainly used by the convenience of mafia Drug Cartels via segregation making it easy to dump on Black communities and to turn them into the hands and feet of the Cartels. It was not that difficult because all a bully had to do is put one person in debt at time whether Black or White, put a poor man into debt with little to no people who have his back and you make them choose slavery or death, and that is how it happens. People choose slavery, because they technically are not hurting anyone. Many people wouldn't choose to be a slave to a Master who orders them to harm someone, but if it is simply to make money and for selling a medicine that people like, and they are simply taking a jail risk with the other option being death, well, people choose to take the risks; they also can make a little money at it, and some of them ended up and end up liking that aspect, and there is that is the

obvious way of how the gangs began to grow. NOTE: You see that the origin of the Cartel dealing gangs did not likely start via seeking it out by choice = It came to them via a swindle to start with, then by threat the first time anyone would come up short on money, and don't forget that they were under threat of silence for fear of being caught and threats to not let any information out about who their supplier was. Some of that happens today, but much of today's is such a trickle effect - that process is not as common, but is on a smaller scale of severity (the secrecy risks), but much larger market.

134) The drug free side of society exasperates the problems by having a prejudice segregation stance. I say "prejudice" because the segregation is good to keep a drug free side of society, but they should not be prejudice about it, which brings isolation and no realistic psychological help approaches instead of simplified segregation for safety reasons.

135) Much of the drug free side of society including religious Christians will talk about the people in communities that are overrun by Cartels as if they don't matter, and "who cares", because "if they didn't learn right growing up then they will never learn". Some say about those who go to "Juvenile Detention" that "if they didn't learn right before age 13 then it is too late". People in drug free societies say that "if they were in a drug area and got shot - they knew that is expected to happen there." Police use to often say that "drugs is all there is in these communities" and would strongly direct anyone from not around there out of there.

136) It has been well known by Police and society that certain areas are heavy drug areas, and that the clean neighborhoods are clean neighborhoods, but even though Police and everyone else generally knows where the drug areas are they have remained drug areas.

137) How have Police known for decades where the drug areas are while media succeeded at sending out a double message of abstaining from drugs mostly in drug free zones while secretly supporting drugs in other areas of society? Well, legislators as influenced by top politicians who had Cartel connections had made laws that make it difficult for Police to gather any evidence without a warrant, and they made it difficult for Police to get warrants for drug searches. Most Police use to be from drug free zones and did not have a hateful view of people involved in drugs, although some did, but simply had a practical view in thinking that drugs are not good for people, but Police generally had not known about all the Political conspiracies that I speak of, and how drugs were unfairly pressured on to

many people including and perhaps most often young people who would just deal with life based on what is in front of them more than an adult would, although, adults often do the same. Now, I know a lot of White people who would get angry at this and say, "you are just sitting here trying to excuse people for their wrongs", NO, I am saying they don't even know what is right and wrong on the issue, and frankly you - my accuser - does not really know what is right and wrong on the issue either, you just think you do. By the way, I am not excusing, I am seeking ways of reconciliation and solutions versus condemnations with no resolutions.

138) I will reiterate here that many things happened per chance such as, lawyers trying to make money by promoting bail and pay outs while that has led to various ways that the system likes making money off of Cartels bailing people out, and high up Cartels associated with top politicians and political interest groups have influence legislation to make money off the Cartel system via the Prison system and Justice system. There are so many loopholes, it is all hard to keep up with, but that led to the race baiting game, which by many is used to protect the path of Cartel business from Police who still enforce drug laws. Some Black people know it is all a game and others fall for the Democrat Media's tricks and actually hate all the supposedly racist White people while not realizing that they themselves are the racist who cannot see past their own racism to detect tricks and lies. Many Black people in the Drug Cartels play along with the racism game while knowing full well they are just promoting segregation to protect their drug cartel businesses, and they know that most White people simply mind their business, go to work, church, restaurants, home and exercise living in peace with people. They even know that the truly racist White people are often their Drug Cartel partners and are not typically the people who work regular jobs, and are not Police, but they just don't like Police interfering with their money flow and the threat of losing their freedom for a time. The sentencing standards need improving so as to be fair and create less tension between Police and various offenders. Police should focus most on detouring assault and theft.

139) How do I think that America has had the largest Drug Cartel in the World when it is seemingly not highly organized? Because, America has likely had the most drug markets with the highest number of small markets that mirror the free market system, and cartels take tips from the free-market system, but have worked overall like an Anarchy by nature. America has a lot of success with our free-market system, and our government's social programs naturally help recycle people back into the free-market system which complimentary to business, including underground business. People like to have a social life on weekends, and

the temptations, curiosities and demands simply renew. I may be wrong in thinking other Nations may not have had the same process happening, but America certainly took a lead in Media worldwide and promoted the underground culture worldwide that we have had here in America. So, I think that America has had enormous numbers of small underground markets feeding from a mass supplier via Mexico's Cartels, and small marketers in America seem to have branched out around the world and spread the small underground more content market system process throughout the World and there are likely only a few very large suppliers and perhaps medium sized suppliers have grown also to keep up with all the smaller markets. Some people may be angered by talking about this so nonchalantly, but that is the way it is - why pretend it does not exist, it is outgrowing the drug free World very quickly, and the people in the culture are tired of the ignorance, because the culture of medicinal users are not as bad as they are painted out to be, but the business side of it is laced with too much swindling and paranoia, which reaps violence in my assessment and many impulsive unwise life decisions.

140) PROBLEMS OF NO REGULATION WITHIN THE CARTEL WORLD: Many problems exist in the underground Drug Cartel world. There are various groups who think it is cool to steal, and they even get so greedy or proud of being a bully that they will steal a car from their own customer or friends. What happens when a person's car gets stolen? Well, they may have also lost their job. Why do many Cartels have such bad business practices? Well, who knows exactly, it really does not make sense, except that Democrat media has trained many people to be extremely prejudice that last 35 to 40 years or so. I suppose people are angry at their risks of going to jail, and angry that if they are in the drug dealing game and don't have a job that they cannot have a savings account, so they just get thrills from gifting themselves with something they want to steal now and then or a few sales to party with over the weekend. Other groups like to make slaves out of their customers by crediting them a product and running up their debt before they have sobered up and charging high amounts of interest, and then many of them threaten to have ALL the money by a certain amount of time and they insist that there is no grace period and that they cannot come to pay them if they are short of the whole payment. What is the purpose of that? Why threaten people's lives? When people's lives are threatened and they can only realistically pay partial payments for a time, then why risk scaring someone off into another State? Why not let people handle other bills they have? The answer to that is that sometimes they are just being a bully, and other times it is because they want a person to go insane, and join the business side of things instead of simply being a medicine consuming customer.

The reason for having high interest rates is to keep a person trapped so that they have a regular customer who cannot afford to quit or go anywhere else. Those things are very common in the Cartel World. I will say that they are not highly common, because there are many people who won't play the credit debt game on people for various reasons, but there are some people who will take those risks or conveniences depending how they look at it or do it. I am not sure if the credit debt thing is viewed as favorable in most cultures or not. I tend to think that most people in the drug culture do not view putting people into high interest credit debt or any debt where the dealer is impatient as a fair thing, and other people in the cultures don't like it because a dealer can complain and not give props to other users while blaming one or two people that owe them and they can try to get a whole bunch of people angry at those they claim debts on, even if most of the debt is interest and not a real debt. Well, killing person does not help to receive a payment from that person, and making a person too afraid to walk down the street to go to work does not help that person's ability to pay off a debt; it hinders it.

God's ten commandments should be promoted and expected across cultural lines despite regulated business or not. God's ten commandments are human rights, and they actually help the ability for doing good business and having better livable results for the whole circle of life.

141) Back to the LBGTQ factor and also the "Feminist interest groups" factor. I mention "Liberal Feminist groups" because they are often related to the L in LBGTQ, population control groups, and many of them appear to be in the "Antifa" groups. I let these groups off a little easy earlier on in this book, and I am not out to demonize anyone who is simply out to defy the medicine laws when they have the knowledge that medicine is medicine and realize that the laws are pretty dumb or conspiring, but I do oppose people oppressing other people unfairly; and frankly, I think that parts of the LBGTQ and some feminists as well as population control activists know a little more about the conspiracies behind the Science and psychology of various drugs imposed on the Ghettos versus drugs used by Hollywood and more upper class groups. I also think that many Black Cartels had graduated up long ago to become aware of the whole drug map and impacts of the character of each drug when used in swindler forms with swindlers pressuring consumers. The psychology of swindling people who use medicine products and basically rushing people who use medicine is not a good way to use medicine. Any medicine should be used only a little bit at a time most of the time except when in extreme pain. My point here is not to delve into that psychology, but is that LBGTQ sectors who are associated with high-ranking American Cartels are often aware of

all these things, and I mentioned earlier that they tend to know when government is going to do a gentrification project in a drug war torn Ghetto. I will also say that many of the LBGTQ activists are NOT LBGTQ people, but are Communists and sometimes KKK or Black Panthers, and there are also Muslim people high up in the know with high ranking "American Drug Cartel". My leaning is that there are many LBGTQ people who hide behind the LBGTQ and are high ranking Cartel members and are big into helping shuffle the larger pure amounts of cocaine powder and meth powder forms to both the poor communities via getting them to powder dealers in Black communities and meth dealers in poor white communities while many LBGTQ people are likely doing more direct deliveries of more pure powder forms to the rich and wealthy in Hollywood and other wealthy party crowds. That is my notion, and it makes sense, and it is not intended for drug busting purposes, but is intended to show that although the Ghettos have a humongous number of small markets - they are not the main runners, even though they are probably the main voice used to call it racist to oppose "The American Drug Cartel", and the politics running the formula that runs "The American Drug Cartel" are the one's playing the racist game to forcefully facilitate the whole thing and that is not the LBGTQ's doing either - it is the politics of Democrats for a long time in favor of supporting Communist regimes and slave regimes in opposition to the free market system under God. I cannot say if it is White Supremacist motivated, because Black Supremacists also like Communism. I am just now analyzing whether the LBGTQ is a victim just like the Black American population has been a victim of the regime in general, and I would say that "yes, I think the LBGTQ is also partly a victim", but some LBGTQ are players who love communism just like some Black racists are players who love communism, and just like some White supremacists and atheists and Muslims and other false religions are players who like Communism. "The American Drug Cartel" leaders were likely in the business mostly for the money and only grew to a point of partnering with the government regimes by the Democrats who have continued to do them favors, and clearly one reason that Democrats like globalism is because they are making money off "The American Drug Cartel" worldwide and they want to continue to use that in favor of them attaining a Global supremacy government. Frankly, I have a notion that the primary "Drug Cartel" leaders in Mexico and America are not thrilled or fully on board with the Democrat Politicians Globalism regimes, but I am not sure, that is just my notion, because the original crooks are those in government who influence the legislation that made natural medicines illegal, and although Cartels benefit financially from that - they don't benefit in a way that is peaceable because of the crooked laws - so, I kind of doubt they fully like the laws. The bad laws are in a sense what has made the Cartel leaders a slave to double standards despite them benefiting, but mostly only benefiting financially.

142) There are racists in the God hating sectors of the LBGTQ activist groups; that is not a surprise because anyone who opposes the God of one human race is by its true natural definition a racist.

143) BIG PART OF CARTEL FORMULA - PERHAPS THE BIGGEST PART: All of the false accusations of racism against Black people is the apparent largest part of "The American Drug Cartel" formula. Yes, the Democrat Party is dumping problems on the Black community; they have been imposing problems on the Black community for years and calling freedom loving people racist, and many Black Americans have fallen for taking out their anger on the innocent bystanders that the Democrats holding Black Americans hostage falsely place the blame on. Unfortunately, Democrats have devised a system that has been dumping Cartel problems onto many Black communities for so long that some in the Black community are dependent on the Cartel, but call it racist for people to point that out, because they are vulnerable either way. Basically, they are screwed. They are angry that people don't point out they have been sabotaged, but they are also angry if you point out their sabotage because that identifies many of them as being part of "The American Drug Cartel", but take my word for it - that lifestyle was literally dumped on them - and I even disagree with one of my favorite people named Ben Carson that people caught up in that system have no one else to blame but themselves. I agree with Ben Carson to a point = Ben Carson got out when he could before he got too deep, but it is nearly impossible for a lot of people who were caught deep in it to get out right away. I will not say it is impossible, but sometimes it absolutely takes a process and time to work one's way out if they are too deep in it. Some people have to pay a debt to get out, other people cannot get out because too many people fear they know too much and simply won't let them out (only in some circles where people are paranoid). There are also factors such as those who have some addiction issues and relapses making it hard to pull away from people who will actually stalk them down; the best ways to get away from those situations is often to move to another town if possible.

144) Many religious Christian Americans add to the problem, because there is a lot of "legalism" in the religious communities who believe all their successes come from living in drug free environments. Many often believe their work ethic and habits are what brings their good success and they

judge everyone according to having or not having the same kind of habits and work ethics. Well, legalism is basically the Pharisee lifestyle that Christ strongly opposed in the New Testament.

145) Here is how the Christian Pharisee lifestyle is a problem to the Black communities affected by the "Democrat Party Drug Cartel" otherwise known as "The American Drug Cartel". A lot of Pharisees tend to pick on people for living in Public housing and they begrudge people government help. Well, I go a step further and I think the government help should even be more invested in investments. What I mean is that why let the dollar go to waste by having people pay half rent and HUD or whatever government venue pay the other half and then they never own it. If it is all going toward rent and then they are still later on homeless then what good is that. If the government is paying rent for them the rest of their lives, then what good is that so far as the dollar goes? THE POINT is that it should RENT TO OWN - so, what if we are helping somebody, we should be wanting the tax dollar to be an investment and help someone. They are paying part of the rent out of their pocket whether it is social security money or not and you should want it to be an investment rather than going it simply disappearing. If you don't want it paying for the whole price, then the government can pay long enough to help them with the down payment and then they can assume the mortgage payments with hope and a new found job. The benefits are multiple = The government would no longer be paying for that property; that person could opt to rent out their own house later on and buy another house and the person they are renting to or selling to may be a person who would have otherwise lived in government housing; the next homeless person in line for housing is now able to come off the street and start the same process and you have created more free market rental business rather than turning government into a rental business; you have now lowered the rental prices in the free market because free market apartments may now buy government housing and turn it into free market rentals or Condominiums; and sometime it can be a rent to own Condominium for the person living in a government housing unit. In the end there still may be more temporary government housing being built, but that is because the previous government housing facilities became free market owned, and then there would not be as much homelessness, violence or long lines for housing and that would leave more help with down payments and security deposits to let people into housing, and once poorer people are in housing it is not that difficult to pay the monthly rent - the security deposits are usually the difficult thing to come up with for people in the streets as they are often surrounded by hustlers or have been paying for storage, or have debts and other issues including medical issues. Frankly, the government rentals are part of the competition with the

free market and doing more rent to own and having less government housing would help drive rental prices down in the free market. The housing costs would be a separate thing, but really it is ideal to have lower rental costs so as to save money toward buying a home.

146) Here is something that Scientists directly benefiting from the Drug Cartels also naturally appear to directly influence. President Trump has recently worked on lower medical drug prices. Think about how Scientists have taken advantage of health insurance from both free markets and government insurance to enormously raise the price of medicines. They charge thousands of dollars for some medicine for a 30-day supply and less. There is nothing fair or rational about that, and they do not cost that much to make, although due to the price gauging the people making them now may charge that much to make them, but that can be changed and it is an unfair price. Well, why would they think of charging that much? Because, they make so much money off of the street drugs that are often stolen from consumers, which causes them to buy more - that Scientists realized or felt they should also jack up the prices of legal medicines as a swindle much the same, because many people are dependent on them and they can simply be stealing from insurance companies. The problem with directly price gauging insurance companies is that people are not dependent on insurance companies to be able to afford any medicine, and insurance companies are rarely if ever able to offer rebates to people who have never needed their service, because of the medical price gauging. Insurance companies are not covering a lot of people that they could cover if Scientists hadn't exploited the system and participated in perhaps the largest price gauging in existence aside from how much some Democrat leaders have made for giving a political speech.

147) SOME NEGATIVE THINGS HAVE A DOMINO EFFECT AND THEN NEGATIVE SCHEMES TAKE ADVANTAGE: When Democrats have pushed God and His ten commandments out of Courtrooms and Prisons then you get longer sentences because the "Golden Rule" is ignored, and then you have Prisoners in jail longer for petty crimes, and God is not revered in some Prisons and Drug Cartels then got a stronger notion to train people for the Cartel within the Prisons and to make more money that way. You also have anti-American Politicians promoting Islamic groups inside the Prisons when there is not natural reverence for the only proven God who rose from the dead. People end up comparing crimes and promote abuse of prisoners with crimes they disagree with while all the while ignoring that they are all supposed to equally be reconciling starting in the Courtroom at their sentencing date and they are not supposed to be measuring one another by their crime, but they are supposed to be

working on repentance, peacemaking, and putting their crimes behind them.

148) People should not be trained to engage in Cartel activity while in reconciliation. They should have incentive to stay busy learning ethics from the Bible, good peacemaking habits, be working on their health, have some work programs to help them save money and/or pay back debts, and they should have a good job search engine within each detainment facility.

149) The Democrat Party has always been the anti-God Party of slavery, Communism and any oppressive regime they can come up with, and that is why they push for immorality and false religions within Prisons toward hoping to brainwash people into supporting various dividing groups in society once they are released from reconciliation. They also do it for the simple reason of silencing truth and reality as a viable message, but truth and reality are the primary messages any sane government should want their Prisoners to learn while in reconciliation before reuniting with the general public.

150) ANALYSIS - WHAT IF EVERYTHING WERE LEGALIZED? These types of questions have not been debated in a long time, and there are some legitimate points on each side of the debate. The problem I have with the side who is against legalizing is that many of them yell and scream and never have a rational discussion about the issue. They are arguing mostly from either a deluded standpoint of thinking that medicine is the devil, or they may actually be hypocritically in favor of the illegal Cartel business by keeping things illegal. Either way, when they are yelling and screaming and making the rational thought look like it is totally crazy or conspiring - I will say once again - that irrational approach might be a scam in favor of Cartels, Prisons or that person may be a hypochondriac or really think that medicines are the Devil. I will say that I certainly think there has to be rules of caution either way.

Frankly, it is almost as if illegal drugs are legal in the segregated Cartel dominated sectors of society, and it has been like that for a long time. If you consider that legalizing everything would really be about the same accessibility that already exists with the illegal markets then it is clearly better to legalize everything for many reasons. If you don't believe that illegal drugs are already that accessible and that legalizing everything would make them immensely more accessible and more tempting then many would oppose it. But the reality is that drugs are already readily available in the illegal markets, and really this is the first time I have looked at it from this perspective. My take has regularly been to legalize the minimal low potency medicine forms, because that is the unquestionably right thing to do in that it acknowledges what a medicine is versus demonizing some of the best natural medicines and putting them in swindler forms with no legal alternatives = that is a scam and it is predatory.

I acknowledge it would be a difficult jump to try to make a case for legalizing everything and that is not my approach, but I do reconsider it from time to time because when you only legalize the weakest medicine forms then the Cartels will possibly still be in nearly full fledge business and the detainment debates and correctional measure to assess will still be an issue, but perhaps those debates and sentencing standards could be far more rational, in part because of books like this, which bring the ethical clarity from the Bible of "Love your neighbor as yourself" into the subject.

What would be my guess of domino effects if everything were legalized? Well, the problem with legalizing everything is that there will still be people who promote drug use for the wrong reasons and will likely market it strongly and do it for money reasons legal or not. On the other hand, if it is all legal then it is not coming at you on the street where you feel some dealers want to ambush you for money if you turn them down to buy their drugs. People will not be fighting and killing over drug money like they do now, and people will not be holding people hostage to secrecy for fear of getting caught to go to jail over drugs. There are a lot of positives about legalizing everything because without the violence associated with illegal dealing there is less pain, and you have a selection of products to choose from without being in a hurry instead of some street dealers pushing the biggest money makers on you to swindle you. Therefore, if they were all legal, I suspect it would be like alcohol sales = Most people won't choose the heavier products, because it is not being pushed on them, and they will choose the smoother products that simply take off the edge like a medicine is supposed to do when properly used.

Okay, what about my Christian views? My Christian view promote abstinence first, but also promote education and recognize that people who completely forbid medicines, which include alcohol are not giving a full Biblical interpretation. The Bible strongly warns that it is not wise to look upon strong drinks (Proverbs 23), and you can clearly compare strong drinks to any medicine because that it what it is. But the Bible also has verses particularly in Proverbs 31 that acknowledge the use of medicine (strong drink) for pain on your death bed, and "wine for those who are heavy hearted and to drown the sorrows of poverty" - in other words times of depression. It does mention that "it is not for Kings to drink so that they don't pervert justice."

There is other Scripture in the New Testament in Ephesians 5:18-33, which tells us "not to be drunk with wine in excess but to be filled with the Spirit singing in Psalms, Hymns and Spiritual songs to the Lord." It is funny or odd how religious people today always re-interpret that to say never to drink wine, and that excess does not mean it is okay to drink a little instead of a lot, but somehow means not to ever drink. Okay, I am not saying it is wise to even drink a little, but it is clearly unwise to think you can control any more than a little if you are set on staying away from drunkenness, and have ever had a problem with it. But today's society has really perverted this issue in favor of complete abstinence and made it into an unpardonable sin to drink or take medicines while simultaneously promoting caffeine products. Any type of drug presents a form of drunkenness, people call alcohol effects a drunk and drug effects a high, but really it is all a form of drunkenness or buzz, and a buzz while preventing drunkenness is the proper medicinal approach when using things for depression. But ACTUALLY YES, the Bible literally says it is okay to drink stronger drink when on your death bed, and it says in Proverbs 31 to drown your sorrows when your heart is heavy - so, I don't know if that means buzz or drunk, but really a buzz is enough to make a person forget their sorrows. ALL THAT SAID - I promote abstinence, nutrition, exercise, prayer and music - while using any medicine form as a last resort only. I do think that I don't feel as prayerful when I have caffeine in me; I don't feel as meditative when I have caffeine, and I prefer to be completely sober from any medicine and to have a more meditative mind with an ability to be more in tune with God, but that still does not happen if we do not put away anger and forgive people and repent of stressful feelings also.

Romans 14 and 1 Corinthians 10 address that we should not eat or drink things in front of weak Christians or people who might be offended by it. Some interpret one of those verses as to never do it at all even on your own time for the sake of those who may not understand. I am not going to revisit that passage and re-assess right now, but I never had a conclusion on it before, I have seen it both ways, but I think my last glance at it had me thinking it was meant to say not to do things in front of a person that might tempt them or offend them. I need to re-assess later and decide if Paul indicated that he would never do it at all even on his own time for the sake of other people, and frankly, I think he may have meant it that way, but by way of his preference and advise for redeeming time and planting more seeds I presume, but not as law or a sin; howbeit, there is also a verse that says, "he that knows to do good and does it not - to him it is sin." My point is that it is not a sin to drink according to Scripture and even according to Paul, but if it is getting in the way of you helping to encourage someone particularly and you choose that over encouragement then that is a sin to you. (don't conclude based on my interpretation, my interpretation is still going to be re-reviewed in depth by me and maybe more again after my next review of those passages)

I think it good to educate ourselves about good nutrition today, because of our fast pace and our bodies that have been medicine trained from growing up in a caffeine induced society. Enjoying good nutrition is about the best way to break away from any medicinal withdrawals. Frankly, a medicine called Tylenol can help a person to get through the headache withdrawal phase when trying to stay off caffeine, and Tylenol does not have any obvious withdrawals, but has negative side effects with too much use like any medicine including caffeine.

It is often hard to think clearly and realistically outside the box when society has drilled you your whole life about how wrong something is, and you catch a glimpse of reality and realize what they said may not be true, but you are a little afraid to think that you are right and they are wrong because you cannot fully explain your realization yet. But here goes. I do feel a bit of an epiphany right now, and I think that having everything legal in the medicine world and highly regulated would clearly be far better than the same products not being regulated while still being made readily available through paranoid swindlers markets. THAT seems to make sense until people start yelling, "how dare you say it should be legal where my children can get to it!" and then they say, "don't you know that more young people will be trying that stuff if it is legal and that many more people will get hooked on those things?" Well, if they are right then I agree with them, but no one can be certain that is correct. It is possible that more young people get hooked in the current format, and that more people who try the medicines get more hooked in the current format due to segregation and other things.

Well, I have been called the anti-Christ and Devil and a promoter of drugs and all kinds of things for trying to discuss a healthier way for society to approach the drug issues full circle. The reality is that I am right to be trying to think of ways to help what is clearly a bigoted segregated system that compliments a lot of violence, theft, hate and is lacking in reconciliation and God's human rights laws. I don't think that highly regulated legal forms would lead to more people or more youth getting on drugs, I actually think it should lead to less, in part because pain creates the wanting for medicines, and a legal system would create a society with far less pain ideally, and the problem is that I can say ideally, but I also think I can say likely, which favors that the legalizing theory. Legal regulation could have laws with some stronger products that don't legalize them for anyone under age 24, and the fact is if some of those regulated products were to hit the streets they would be tested for consistency and in a better form than the current street forms, and people would be lesser inhibited about going to rehab and lesser inhibited about going to help if they have been robbed or ambushed. When you review the obvious it certainly favors a legal more responsible system, which more strongly opposes theft and assault over someone's person management choices of how they use medicine, or how they stay off medicine. A liquor store does not force people to buy their products and drink, but in an illegal medicine Cartel culture there is Anarchy and thieves masked as dealers who impose things on people and people sometimes feel like "if I don't cooperate then I will be ambushed", yes, those things happen pretty regularly and some stand up for themselves and fight an unnecessary fight that would not exist in a legalization society. But there is certainly a question as to whether Democrat and Republican congress would put the proper regulations in place and if Scientists would create the best products but they should be better than the swindler products if they don't delay so as to keep it in the Cartels hands.

   Fast forward to a conclusion on legalizing drugs and I am at a point where I have a confident stance in promoting the legalizing of all street drugs in a 2% potency pill form only and by prescription only, and I believe that gives people who have been pre-exposed to swindler drugs a safe option and an option to not be manipulated by the street game life and to have a more open door to rehabs instead of rehabs being an oppressive thing and locking people down who have already been locked down and robbed by street Cartel swindling games while having to be paranoid and segregated by the predatory laws imposed on medicine consumers, which include medicine consumers who are caught with a fairly small amount of drugs being charged as a dealer at times when that is not the case. I believe the 2% form is a proper medicine form that is in line with Biblical advice on medicines.

The swindling games in conjunction with the Pharisee views in society, which exist on the segregated drug free side of society cause people to feel very imprisoned particularly when the Pharisee side of society and the Cartels are all benefiting off of the compromising tricks of the system and the consumers who get robbed are those who are regularly exposed in the hateful segregation debates. That gives some perspective, and many people are like "who cares - they should just leave that life alone", well, that is what is being discussed here; I am discussing the ways to help people out of the traps that have been set in the current system, and people who have never been cross cultural people are not likely to understand especially if they are cold hearted people, and this book is for the sake of God's vision of "loving our neighbors as ourselves" regardless of what their stumbling block is, and I am discussing some systematic and conspiring traps that have been created on a large scale based on lies about medicine that the cold hearted actually love, because many cold hearted Pharisee types actually make their living and survival by keeping a high position from oppressing other people and making them look bad in order to ensure they have no competition, and at other times simply for their own pride sake, but a lot of people are left isolated for societal predators and are killed thanks to Pharisee types who are in support of the exact illegal drug stance that the most greedy Cartels support. The fact is that the most greedy and violent sectors of the Drug Cartels oppose legalizing just the same as the Pharisee critics who pretend that drugs are the Devil and should stay completely illegal. You have to wonder at times if those Pharisees also play hypocrite and are part of the Drug Cartels as beneficiaries, then in a way, they do benefit from others peoples calamity in the system just the same.

151) Why hate on drug dealers by the way. They are just people like anyone else = You know the human beings that Jesus refers to as neighbors that we are supposed to love as our self. Everyone was not taught the same things growing up. The best governing methods we can all teach each other and learn to conform more to are God's simple ten commandments for loving neighbors by respecting the right to life and right to private property among other things.

152) How do I feel about Drug Cartel swindlers markets, and the people who do the swindling? Well, I look at it like this. I oppose stealing and swindling, but I also understand that a corrupt government system on the Democrat Party side and their media have brainwashed people into thinking that stealing is a false religious law used for rich and powerful people called "White Supremacists" for the sake of putting poor people in jail, and at one time just Black people in jail who needed money and went out to steal because "White Supremacists" would not give them any real jobs and imposed the drugs in their society and lock them up if they are caught dealing them while at the same time they funnel the drug money back to themselves (the Supremacists).

Well, my point is that is very similar to what many people who grew up around drug cultures learned as Democrat groups lied to them over and over again. Clearly, "thou shalt not steal" is a natural universal law that protects every single person individually and it is a right to happiness law that comes straight from God. So, the Democrat political scheme lied to Black people mostly and told them that stealing was a racist law (they now teach White Cartel cultures the same things), and so I understand that many Black people in the swindling cultures were taught that and that is the means they understand for survival and they actually have honor among each other by respecting one another's property and they mostly have swindling rules that swindle people who like to party and do not handle intoxication well while actually body guarding some of those types of people in return. So, much of them have a conscience and feel locked into the system by no real choice of their own. However, people can get greedy and do overkill in those settings as well, but books like this one could help solve some of those problems in the future or in future generations and help to put a lot more people on a level playing field - no one is beyond God-Christ-Spirit's forgiveness and redemption regardless. Lying political leaders and media liars are those who need the most rebuke for lying to entire cultures and masses of people. Religious Pharisees also need to be rebuked in favor of true compassionate Christianity.

153) I will reiterate here that it is safe and rightful and is in line with Biblical cautionary advice to offer legalized medicinal form low potency products of street medicines in 2% potency pill for by prescription only. Doing so also burst the lying illusion that demonizes medicines and recognizes that medicines can have low potency more conservative forms and also stronger forms of the same medicines. The stronger forms of any medicine can create an uncanny drunkenness.

153) WHAT IS THE DRUG CARTELS PERSPECTIVE ON LEGLIZATION? Well, much of the Drug Cartel likely do not want to lose their business to licensed dealers, but there are many people in the Drug Cartel cultures who may see the benefits of having some legal forms and are tired of the laws that imprison people for non-violent crimes.

154) Understand how large drug cultures are. Basically, when you look at the fans of today's secular music scenes and see millions and millions of people and most of them tend to vote Democrat. Well, it is in part because they favor the Drug Cartel cultures politics that are promoted by Democrats, Hollywood and many Musicians. There is a mix of reasons people choose those politics, such as being told that opposing false religion is bigotry, or being told that people who oppose killing babies hate women, or being told that opposing same sex marriage is hate for gay

people, or being told that a border wall is racist against Mexicans. Well, a lot of people simply fall for those lies, and are not into the drug cartel culture, but may sympathize with drug cartel culture in that they know many people go to jail for non-violent crimes in the marijuana side of the culture, and somehow Democrats convince people that they are the friend to people who are oppressed by some of those compromising situations. By the way, Democrats are hypocritical in that they created the predatory drug laws in the first place, and are known for the KKK demonizing drugs years and years ago, which is what created the prohibition laws versus having a regulated system. Democrat leaders are also hypocritical in that Eric Garner who died in New York City a few years ago, while being detained by a choke hold was arrested because of a new Democrat created law that outlawed the selling of cigarettes in New York (it may have been a Nationwide law, I am not sure). Anyhow, the Drug Cartel Cultural influence is humongous whether the young Democrat voters support some Democrat Politics because of them or not, they are certainly influenced by those who protect the Drug Cartels. Frankly, BLM and Antifa the NBA and Beyonce', Jay-z, and T.I, and Madonna and many others in their war against Police is all in part to protect the Drug Cartels free flow of illegal business. You have to wonder instead of spreading all that hatred, why don't they simply push for legalization? Because they actually like the swindling and thieving groups that push their products, and many other not so good reasons.

155) WHY DOES ALL THIS MATTER? For many reasons, but it turns out I am showing you that "The American Drug Cartel" is made up of many people who do not exactly view themselves as Cartel, but as victims to a prejudice society that has surrounded them with drug activity while simultaneously outlawing it. Many people around Drug cultures are there from many different situations. Some were smuggled into the Country as children, some just grew up around it, others had parents who were "addicts", others had friends that were involved in it, some ran into it at the clubs, others had their drink spiked at a club and were introduced to it that way, others gravitated to it because they were told that people who oppose drug culture are bigots (and some are, but there are dangers to drugs also), some men fell for a woman who was in it, women fell for a man that was in it, some people joined it for the money, and other people ran into it from pain or a tragedy.

156) There is a problem with Democrats who lie about Police and are not candid about what they support, and they always lie about people being racist and they never offer any solutions to societal problems. The Drug Cartel is a business, and people like the NBA who lie to create formulas

that use the Drug Cartel as a pawn are not really friends to the Drug Cartel business, but are more like the slave master formula that has put the Drug Cartel in the compromising position they are in. Lies are bad, assault is bad, and lies that support many assaults and much thievery are evil conspiracies. The problem starts with the Political conspirators, which include the NBA and Sports media. Why are athletes so invested in these evil conspiracies? Are they directed by media? Sports media certainly has a strong influence, but many NBA players may see themselves on the rich side of things and want to create an extreme rich and poor class where the poor class has no policing and the rich class has paid policing. Why would NBA players want that? Well, they are more familiar with Drug Cartels than they pretend to be = They see the rich class Cartels in the mix of their Hollywood partying involvement and some of them have said they grew up around the Ghetto Drug Cartels. Perhaps NBA players don't know a lot about the Political end, but simply follow a basic message, or maybe they just feel that the Drug Cartels will never go away so they want to accommodate them to help run the poor side of Society in a very rich and very poor split society that they are supporting via Social Communism in the future. It is hard to know and understand why NBA players are so dedicated to a deadly cause.

157) WHAT SHOULD THE CHRISTIAN CHURCH STANCE BE WITH DRUG CARTELS? The Christian Church should generally be sending out a clear message to the entire public including people involved in Cartels that Christ is the God of forgiveness and redemption, and that Christ is opposed to a life of thieving, assault and sexual activity outside of marriage between man and woman. Christ teaches us to "treat others the way we want to be treated", and commands everyone to "love their neighbors as themselves". I will discuss Christian principles in more detail later, but Christians should walk in forgiveness, with Spirit fruit and truth.

158) WHAT SHOULD THE POLICE STANCE BE WITH DRUG CARTELS? I propose two separate Police forces. I propose the "People's Police", which protects people rights from God's ten commandments and include the rights to private property and the rights to life without being assaulted; and I propose that there be a separate "Drug Force" Police unit, because the Police who protect people's rights should do so without partiality due to drug issues. It is ideal for Police to have good Biblical knowledge and to be pro-life versus pro-abortion murder.

159) Think about how much of a bully the NBA players are when they use lies 100% of the time, and won't back off their lies and demonize anyone who believes in "One Nation Under God", and they absolutely will not give

one bit of credit to where credit is due to any of their political enemies, and they promote "The American Drug Cartel". You know what that means to me? It means they run "The American Drug Cartel" as their soldier for slavery. It means that "The American Drug Cartel" can do no wrong in their eyes. It means that no matter how many people "The American Drug Cartel" murders in Chicago - their lives have no relevance and don't matter, because the only thing that matters is their power of lies.

Now, I am using the NBA as the model example because they are so unified in their lies and hate, but the Sports media connected to Disney, Hollywood and the Democrat media monopoly over "The American Drug Cartel" slavery - well, media have been the leaders, and teachers to the NBA players and other athletes, but the NBA players can no longer be looked at as victim of media lies and neither can anyone else to a degree, because if someone believes their lies and echoes their lies, well it is their responsibility NOT to believe the lies and not to teach hate and to rebuke murder and assault instead of standing up for and promoting more murder and assault, and these people have not acknowledged even one "Antifa" attack - they use a case like George Floyd to pretend they are against violence - but violence, slavery and theft represents everything they stand for in their regular support of "The American Drug Cartel" and opposition to Police, and in their regular support of people such as "Snoop Dogg" and other Hollywood, Music and Movie venues that have been promoting violent sectors of "The American Drug Cartel" for decades. They also promote abortion without any consideration of their stance at all and they promote and support violence against people opposed to abortion.

160) Do I think that "Drop Dead" prayers are ethical or wrong? Well, I think we should love our neighbors, which include enemy neighbors, but I believe in the death penalty for murder, not for self-defense killings in War, fights or in defending someone else in some sets of circumstances, BUT ambush resulting in the victim's death is murder, whereas self-defense resulting in death is not murder unless there was adequate time to calm a situation and the person kills when not necessary after a situation is contained.

Well, when "Repent or Drop Dead" prayers are used to defend and protect people from murderous regimes like the NBA and Democrat media support in supporting "Antifa", and in promoting Black revenge killings on innocent people based on false statistics, killing and harassing Police who had nothing to do with a particular case they claim anger about, killing babies via abortion, and in supporting Chicago killings by "The American Drug Cartel". Yes, I think "Drop Dead or repent" prayers are fitting in order to save more lives by praying for conspirators and their foot soldiers who are killing people, vandalizing and stealing on a regular basis to repent, drop dead or be stopped in some other way.

161) WHAT DO I THINK IS THE BEST SELF DEFENSE IN DRUG CULTURES? Well, it is a matter of preference. I think "repent or drop dead" prayers apply in praying against violent thieving regimes, but do so in hope of repentance and while still loving enemy neighbors, but should you carry a weapon or go without a weapon in high crime settings? Well, sometimes having a weapon is threatening to people and they view it as fighting words and they want to shoot or stab you before you stab them. So, it depends how you carry it, but simply having a weapon triggers some people to contest you. Anyone who considers carrying a weapon should understand that before making their decision. The primary approach to take with people is to let it be known that you are for peacemaking and being a peacemaker whether you are carrying a weapon or not. If you do not carry a weapon and you make it clear you are peaceful, most the time people will not bother you and will let you mind your business but every now and then some person looking to ambush anyone can cross your path and if you don't have a weapon it could be a problem, and that is a risk that some people take - peace talking and negotiation psychology works quite well with people most of the time, but sometimes there are people who want nothing of peace and have an agenda to take whatever they want. I think that usually those extreme situations are quite rare, so the risks of carrying a weapon and it creating a controversy are bigger than not carrying a weapon, but I do believe in having a weapon inside of your home, and that is not a threatening thing, because no one is supposed to be at your home except invited guests, welcomed business, the mailman, the dump truck...

162) Technically, NBA players, Democrat media and Democrat leaders do not deserve to have a car because they promote groups like "Antifa" and some "BLM" rioters who destroy innocent civilian cars. It is one thing to promote "BLM" based on their title, but when you intentionally never rebuke the violence and vandalism of "Antifa" and never rebuke the violence and vandalism of some "BLM" sectors then you are supporting that with your big microphone, and why should you be allowed to have a car if you are destroying innocent people's car and continue promoting that = "An eye for an eye".

163) America's drug rehabs are a big problem and America's homeless shelter drug rehab systems are also a problem. Why? Because they do not support freedom. Now, I understand many of them believe in their

philosophy, but governments view is not about "addiction psychology" and are supporting slave regimes and government dependency in support of a future Communistic Socialism regime that they hope for. The whole rehabilitation system is backwards and religious community's support the backwards philosophies. Whatever the program the goal should be for people to be independent and free, and the problem actually starts with a key motto accepted in nearly the entire rehabilitation World = "Once an addict always an addict." If that were the case and is the philosophy and were truth then what is the point in rehabilitation = "Once an addict always an addict" implies that there is no possibility of rehabilitation; therefore, the foundational philosophy of addiction rehabs in this Country support hopelessness on the issue and imprisoning addicts and forcing them into a live of dependence on group and away from an individual dependence on God, which would allow them the liberty to manage themselves and make their own decisions.

The "once and addict always an addict" philosophy problem simply feeds into the hands of Drug Cartels who are advantaged by making drugs illegal, because the human spirit is still claustrophobic and will play that group game and will have some desired acquaintances from time to time in those settings, but anyone is going to want to break away periodically and should want to and they are likely to find their freedom in the very thing that they are being locked away against, because basically all of their other fresh air freedoms have been stolen from them by a perverted philosophy of life that declares them not free based on a prejudice stereotype that declares medicine use as an unpardonable sin and ignores that the tragedies that come from medicine use is usually due to an illegal swindlers market who robs their customers, but still are representative of the few people in society where a so-called addict can go to escape the prejudice stereotyped tag placed upon them.

The reality of any medicinal physical withdrawal stage is that it only lasts about 3 days or so, and if anyone sticks it out through those withdrawal pains or fatigue, the addiction phase is broken, and the body begins to feel good and a person naturally does not want to go through that process again if they understand that recovery process, but today most people are not aware of that process as they are told they can never overcome addiction, except by being imprisoned to a group. Groups do have some attraction and do help some in that people in groups about medicine can relate to one another on the issue and our society is segregated on the issue, which makes people often feel isolated; but the overwhelming group philosophies are simply wrong and imprisoning.

The argument that "addiction specialists" will make is that there is emotional addiction also. Well, what is wrong with medicine for depression? If a person has a legitimate emotional injury that they know comes on to them at a time they realize they have no hope to access their childhood dreams, such as on a pay date and not having enough money to take two steps; rather than being angry or depressed is it a sin to take a medicine of their choice? Technically, no it is not a sin, the Bible in Proverbs 31 even supports it as an option. Is it the best option? Well, sometimes actually. A medicine is a good option if a person literally cannot control their temper and if it gets them past thoughts of vengeance; sometimes we need to do things including going for a bike ride instead of medicine to get us past some obsessive angry thoughts. Therefore, a so-called relapse does not mean that a person did not make progress in 3 weeks of being clean - those clean days in reality actually count. The problem is that many people like certain medicines and go to risky places run by drug cartels to get their medicines and they are at risk of losing their whole savings when going to a place like that, but that is the only place available for people to be approved to get a medicine with our many crazy and predatory laws set by politicians in the know of the formula, and by deluded politicians also as supported by deluded religious people as their most reliable and respected conscience perverts.

So, one could argue that there is a self-management problem and too strong a desire for a medicine if a person will go to a place where they are in risk of danger or being robbed to get their medicine; and they want to declare a person inept and incapable of self-management if they are willing to take that risk, and that can make some sense if you care less about the principles of freedom and independence but really the people who try to put people like that on lockdown are the reasons that a person would want to run and "get out of Dodge" and go to a risky place where they are escaping being bothered by people who view themselves as "prison keepers" for a change and break. It makes plenty of sense to escape such settings and take a risk, unless people are NOT treating a person like a prisoner, then a person has time for more rational thinking in their decisions rather than thinking - hurry, run and go to the most available hiding spot for a little break, and figure the rest out later.

So, really the prison keeping philosophies created by the rehab and religious perversion worlds are a big part of the problem that also feeds hypocrisy among people in the rehab groups who learn to sneak around and work together to simply find better places to use medicines where they are not as easily robbed and have one another's back and can trick the system. Some people in those groups actually do stay clean and learn to like using language that helps oppress new people and they know how to say words that will influence a "relapse" and they get their fix from digging out the relapse stories from people they helped trip up and sometimes that is pride based and other times it is them believing the bad philosophies and liking to prove the bad philosophies right, but the problem is that they are looking at medicine use as if it is the unpardonable sin, and that being loyal to a clique is the Savior.

The bottom line is that drug rehabilitation philosophies, Cartel philosophies and many religious philosophies all support slave regimes, and frankly the Police have a more freedom complimenting philosophy than all of them. The Police in general say, "stay out of trouble and you don't have to see us - do all you can to stay away from us" - that is a fairly freeing philosophy; the problem with today's enforcement is sentencing standards are way off kilter in various situations, and should mostly target thievery and assault that strongest.

164) "THE AMERICAN DRUG CARTEL" = TADC - technically it is "The Democrat Party Drug Cartel" = TDPDC, but most Americans shortsighted philosophies support it in different ways.

165) "The American Drug Cartel" has a couple of major wrongs. They are basically a slave organization. The Democrat Party has regularly celebrated slavery during February while pretending they are against it - THINK about what is natural to celebrate = THE VICTORY OVER SLAVERY - THE OUTLAWING OF SLAVERY BY ABRAHAM LINCOLN ON HIS FEBRUARY BIRTHDAY MONTH! Whether originally by chance or not - I think the Democrat Party ON PURPOSE has celebrated slavery regularly to anger people about slavery that no longer exists so that people do not recognize the basic defining principles of slavery WHILE they have underhandedly tricked a lot of people into supporting their Drug Cartel slave regime.

One way that real forms of slavery are run is by accepting a lie that someone's property rights are less important than your property rights, which is basically throwing out God's ten commandments. Therefore, nearly any form of slavery is based on a lie about which people are important. All people are important to God in their right to life and rights to private property, and rights to be judged by truth instead of uncontested lies being told about them and judging them accordingly.

A basic principle of extreme slavery is to force people by threatening their life or to facilitate severe punishment if they do not do what they want them to do, and "The Democrat Party Drug Cartel" shows us how they love slavery by using "Antifa" to assault people who do not agree with them. "The Democrat Party Drug Cartel" shows us how they love slavery by using "BLM" to threaten people who do not agree with their racist lies or Communism. By the way "BLM" lies include the lie that Black people can't be racist; well, the Black leaders of "BLM" are racist and are invested in racist Black Panther and Black racist Islamic groups, and Black racist liberation groups who want Black neighborhoods only and Black business only instead of integration.

It is slavery to kill, threaten or batter a person who is late on a payment like many Drug Cartel members threaten to do. It is slavery to force a person to give up their money. That is theft, but also is slavery. Technically, theft is slaving the victim, and slavery is theft. It is slavery to have gang initiations and to threaten people who want to get out of a gang. It is attempted slavery to threaten people physically who don't want to vote for the same person you do. It is not a freedom to vote view that threatens people physically who wear a Trump or Obama hat, and of course it is only Democrats who make those threats and act on them, and many of them do not oppose that violence like they should because of greed or they simply support it = Supporting slavery. The Islamic slave trade in Africa is slavery and the Democrat called people "Islamophobes" who try to contest it, and Democrats are therefore, supporting the Islamic slave trade while pretending to hate on slavery that does not exist and pointing the finger at America for past slavery when that slavery was run by the Democrat Party and they are still angry they were forced to stop engaging in that slavery. It is slavery when Democrats constantly lie about Police attacking Black people when it is Black people attacking Police and Democrats want Police out of Black neighborhoods so that a Black person is scared to walk to work in fear of getting shot by various Cartel culture group people, because the Police do not have any containment there with "The Democrat Drug Cartel" demanding that Police be out of those neighborhoods. It is slavery for Democrat media and Democrat leaders to be lying about Police shooting down Black people randomly - that is not happening and has not been happening and the Democrats do that to make Black people afraid to walk down the street to go to work from fear of being shot, and that joblessness slavery via lies is what Democrats want for Black people, which in turn causes many of them to join a local Drug Cartel safety net instead of finding a legitimate job. Those Democrat lies even result in some people going to a mental institution or turning to drugs to deal with their paranoia's created by lies, but also from lies creating real violence and giving reign to violent gangs in neighborhoods where the Police presence has been rejected. Thanks to some Police who ignore the threats against them - Police in general do not let violent gangs have a complete 100% takeover of neighborhoods so that they don't create a hood that is 100% slave to violent gangs; howbeit, gangs do often succeed at making some hoods between a 40% and 80% slave to their dominance there.

166) Many perhaps most people in the drug culture do not realize they are engaging in slavery, and do not realize that they are slaves. Oftentimes, the case is that they are not full-time slaves, but are part time slaves. In other word's they can go home, but are under threats if they do not come back and fulfill obligations or debts, and those threats on their life or well-being are actually binding them like a slave.

167) Many of the slave Masters in Drug Cartel do not realize that they are performing slavery. Many have been taught the gang or "hustle" culture, and view that as a way of life, and a way of having leaders of a crew, and as being the "top dog" or whatever, and they are respected for it, and women support it in the Drug Culture and Hollywood paints the lifestyle as being sexy and hip, and as one that draws a lot of women; and there are a lot of women involved due to the drugs, and appearing to be like "free birds" in the system rather than housewives, but that is a misconception, because women give up natural freedoms to have other freedoms that are often inconvenient and come with a price but does have various temporary unfulfilling thrills, many of which include living for sin, and need a repentance and reverence for the only supernatural God in Christ who says to "love our neighbors as ourselves" and implies not to use out neighbors as pawns for our own vain selfish gratifications.

168) So, Democrats have used non-existent past slavery as a diversion to trick Black America into supporting Drug Cartel slavery while not recognizing that it is slave style run, and while teaching them that stealing is their right when stealing is part of the main formula for slavery, and while pointing the finger of racism to the Political philosophy of the Republican Party who outlawed slavery and rescued their ancestors from the legalized Democrat slavery at that time. The Republican Party still has the same moral freedom philosophy they had back when they outlawed slavery, but they do not have the right views on medicine and do not know all the medicine tricks that the Democrat Party has played on America and the World, but hopefully this book helps to open some eyes in the Republican Party for ways to fix the system and give people more of their proper freedoms and private property rights and rights to life without so many threats in "The American Drug Cartel" cultures, and hopefully the Cartels wake up to the tricks that manipulate them and have them stealing from their own self while they also rationalize stealing from other people, which

needs to stop whether medicine sales come to a stop or not.

169) NOTE: Not everyone in drug culture is highly abusive; some people do fair business. Doing fair business and treating people right is still good business whether in an illegal drug culture or in regularly grounded culture. It is probably usually the people who do good business that end up capitalizing in the drug culture and then are more in danger of getting into trouble with the law as they become popular. So, some take those risks, and others back out or tap it down. Some decide to take the bigger risks and grow and set up a more violent network around them that sets other people up to take falls for them. Being outside the law in growing a business always creates some kind of negative compromises even for the fair handed business dealers, because they are never safe due to being outside the law. SO, LETS REVIEW ONCE AGAIN - are those good laws or not? Well, when you look at the fact that the most neighborly business persons in the Drug Cartels who engage in fair business are disqualified by the laws - it frankly, makes the laws appear to be irrational, and that medicine dealers should be allowed to have a business license. But I will remind you the cultures that are against that have possible irrational fears that more people would become "hooked" on drugs, but really the perception of "hooked" is frankly given by seeing people who were robbed and are now stuck being homeless, and people think they are homeless just because they are "hooked" on drugs versus realizing they are homeless because they were robbed by various Drug Cartel gangs or gang members.

170) THE WHOLE WORLD IS DELUSIONAL = TWWID = A medicine or drink does not take someone's money. People take other people's money or demand other people's money. A medicine or drink is like ice cream = you may eat one cup and want to buy another cup and the ice cream may cost 5 dollars, but you eat 3 cups and that is 15 dollars, which is getting somewhat costly. A medicine might cost 10 dollars and you may want as much as 5 doses of medicine, which is 50 dollars and that is getting expensive, but the medicine never takes 100 or 200 dollars from a person at a time, only other people do that. People may make a person nervous or be harassing a person who is intoxicated and take their money, but medicines do not cost that much, and a person could even not spend a lot of money on a medicine and over dose. The point is that people who are supposedly "hooked" on drugs are not "hooked" and poor from being "hooked" - there is almost always a swindling network associated with illegal drugs or even other drug consumer partners who are connected to a swindle, and many dealers get greedy also, even though many dealers oppose the swindlers as well.

THE POINT HERE is that legalizing medicines would not render people as homeless like the illegal dealing system does. Matter of fact a lot of housing places kick people out for illegal products and that would not be happening in a legal system either, but rather it would be based on behavior, if anyone is causing problems.

WHAT DO SOME PEOPLE ACCUSE ME OF? Some people automatically assume that I promote legalizing just because I want to be able to use the drugs. That is not the case, and I have never actually been confident one way or the other about whether things should be legal or not - I had only sought the discussions to find the proper answer, but the Pharisee prejudice is so vast that the discussions are hardly possible, and frankly, they don't know what they are talking about and most of them are a bunch of caffeine addicts with ADD on the subject due to the caffeine. That is funny but it is a percentage of the factor of why they have no patience to be realist about ethics.

No, legalization is not a subject that is discussed because people want to be able to have drug access. There is plenty of drug access through various street venues if that is what interests a person, and oftentimes people go to that for a cultural break and not particularly for the intoxication. The problem with the street businesses is that people are expected to use drugs or not bother people whereas, in a legalized society a person is not expected to go to the liquor store just because they are passing by it to go to the Pizza joint next door.

The reason to consider drug legalization is to be rid of the violence and thief networks that pop up around the illegal markets, but frankly, it is time to simply start opposing thievery and violence among Drug Cartels, and just assume they are going to continue the drug dealing part and get caught when they get caught and not get caught when they don't, UNLESS people decide to support the legal venues - then the illegal venues would dwindle.

171) In the Drug Cartel World there are plenty of user dealers also. Some of the user dealers want drug partners and it is typical for some of them to use shaming tactics among people who are not frequent users of drugs. They like to use the rehabilitation philosophies, which believe that it is impossible for any medicine user to be any different from any other medicine user, and they will insist that a person cannot quit among other tactics to harass a person and persuade them to partner with them. Those types will eve steal, gossip and do other things to discourage and depress

or intimidate a person into thinking there is no hope; some might call some of those tactics if taken to an extreme "false imprisoning" - I just call it a control freak trying to hold someone hostage and usually that is for the purpose of bumming or bullying that person's money on the regular and to create a hustle buddy that they want to train. My point here is that in some circles connected to rehabs or in the homeless population there are more of those types lurking around and sometimes they are big time gang recruiters or big-time dealers masked as a drug user while also being a drug user. The problem with those user dealers is that they love the perverted system and love playing on the system, which uses "once an addict always an addict" and they are prejudice against themselves and other medicine consumers and they continue being a promoter of the system, but case and point = those types would hardly exist in a regulated legalized medicine system.

172) In a legalized regulated medicine system - drug rehabs would not be as perverted and rehabs would for the most part have classes to attend that do not interfere with life and jobs, and good nutrition, health and exercise would become a natural course in medicine rehabilitation philosophies.

173) I did not intend for this book to end up promoting legalization of medicines. I had finally settled on simply regularly proposing the legalizing 2% potency forms of medicines in pill form only and by prescription only, but while writing this brief book on "The American Drug Cartel" and reviewing a number of issues surrounding the Cartel drug cultures in one setting instead of in bits and pieces at various times - it simply has become clear to me that the safe and neighborly way for the World of medicine is to have legal venues that are well regulated rather than to let many swindling groups continue to run the medicine World under a paranoid system that results in much violence and jail, which creates fears of jail for non-violent crimes that also create violence. When looking at the Cartel issues as a whole there are simply many more points that show more legalizing with regulation favors more peace and less theft and violence by a huge margin.

174) I cannot see the whole scope of things, but I have covered a lot of issues and solutions for "The American Drug Cartel" to improve and consider legalizing. Now, the reality of what Cartels do not realize is that with legalization their lives will balance out also and there will be more jobs available and better housing options for cheaper because of less crime, and because a lot of illegal drug cases would be dropped. Many felony records would likely be dropped. So, the business lost by many Cartel

sectors would actually turn out to be a gain for many of them also. I understand that many groups, people and families feel they are completely 100% dependent on the Cartels to survive and eat. I do not know the whole scope of that, and I know that some of those groups in no way want to lose their business to legalizing, because they don't have insurance and other investments the same way that people in the grounded lifestyles might, although, other higher up Cartels have made provisions for themselves either way.

I suppose it sounds funny to some that I am sympathizing with people's plans in the Cartel business if street medicines were to have more legal venues, but the Cartel business was mostly created by crooked Science laws and crooked politics so, from my perspective I cannot fully fault a lot of the Cartels, I can mostly only encourage them not to engage in violence and theft, and I can encourage them to get out of the business if they possibly can.

175) Why not sympathize with people? The Bible does support compassion and understanding while still directing people in the ways of truth, God's spirit of eternal peace, and forgiveness. We sympathize with people to make them feel they fit back into the group after they embarrassingly lose their temper if they are a Doctor, Teacher, Preacher, or regular grounded worker. Why not sympathize with the circumstances that herded many underground workers into the settings they are in rather than isolating them as unpardonable so as to limit their apparent survival options to render them only acceptable in the place they are already in that the critics pretend to oppose while simultaneously insistently stereotyping them to only be fitting in that venue? No, I believe in a lesser isolating perspective than that, and making God's redemption path option visible for everyone as the most highly important option of choice we have on this Earth; and that is sensible in every way imaginable.

176) I am an unusual character. I do not think a person in this World has walked in very similar shoes as mine. I have had a strong view of all people being the same since I was fairly young, and I viewed people that way because of my belief that we all came from Adam and Eve equally. Now, that got me into some trouble, but it also gave me a broader look at various cultures than most people I have seen. It got me into some troubles NOT because my view is wrong, but because YES, everyone is the same but everyone is also in a very different place in their mind's perspective and we are even very different in each given day. Also, people have either chosen an eternal peace soul, or an eternal damnation soul, but people's hearts can be consistently wicked or wicked part time. The

eternal peace heart still has to walk in repentance or it can be sour for a time, but a heart that is connected to an eternal damnation soul is always full of greedy games even if it is seemingly peaceful in its loyalty to close friends who accommodate its survival. True faith is a supernatural thing and a person with true faith recognizes the things that connect us as humans and view them in a more peaceful way, but we cannot read the heart, and often cannot know if a person who claims good will or who claims faith is sincere or not. But what we can learn is that God's ten commandments grants us the right to life and our own belongings and we can learn to say no, get away from a situation, or even fight for what is ours, if necessary, when people greedily want what rightfully belongs to us. We can also opt to give things for ransom or for grace purpose and know not to be around the same person who is greedy and covetous the next time, or know to take precaution before communicating with that person again.

177) I would like to remind you that Democrat Party tricks and formulas have been numerous in trapping Black people, poor people, and men. Today, they promote mobs to bully poor people around who do not believe what Democrat leaders want them to believe religiously and otherwise. The Democrats have used Welfare tricks to pay women not to live with their child's father, and made rules that did not allow the father to live in government housing along with their child and mother. That plays into the hand of "child support" corruption. It is actually a lot cheaper for the father and mother to live together and for them to work things out on their own. Child support can be a good thing, but when there is not mercy or more reasonable ways to make payments or to pardon some payments and simply continue where left off or mercy periods and jail is a result, then it often defeats the purpose while jail puts a freeze on the father's income and creates more bills defeating the purpose of child support payments. It is better to have mercy and to keep some level of payments coming in if a father comes up short sometimes, or even regularly is short but is making the effort and getting some money to the mother and child. That is all a part of oppression and when it comes to "child support" flaws in the laws - both Democrats and Republicans are guilty of over doing it on the unreasonableness of the legislation. Courts are also guilty of overcharging and often ruining the purpose.

178) THE DEMOCRATS ARE AGAINST PEACE: In the Democrat Party dealing with "The American Drug Cartel" - it is important to recognize that they are not for peace and never have been. The Democrat Party pretending to sympathize with jail sentencing for non-violent crimes has all been a trick to make people think they care. Understand that the

Democrats have used "The American Drug Cartel" as a way to be a Democrat hand of violence = Democrats PRETEND to be against guns, but they smuggle illegal guns across the border. It is the illegal guns that are used in most murders and in most armed robberies and to force people into slavery. Democrats are going after the legal guns NOT the illegal guns, and the legal guns have a licensing process to regulate that people are using them for self-defense purposes only and are responsible people as best they can - that fact that it cannot be perfect is irrelevant when you compare the good statistics of legal guns protecting against violence and only being used wrongly in very few cases versus the bad statistics of illegal guns used in assault in large numbers.

179) The Democrats have no good intentions when it comes to "The American Drug Cartel", the Cartel exists, and it can be influenced so as to be less violent, but the Democrat media and their leaders refuse to let all the killings in Chicago for example be rebuked and discouraged, and that goes on in every city in America, but the Democrats do not rebuke that violence and they call it racist to rebuke and oppose it. The Democrats do not rebuke the "Antifa" violence they actually promote it.

180) It is important to recognize that "The American Drug Cartel" exists and is technically the largest most active Cartel formula in the World as run by the Democrat Party, their media and interest groups.

181) It is important to encourage "The American Drug Cartel" as a separate entity from the Democrat Party and realize that the Democrat Party influenced laws to sabotage an create the Cartel.

182) It is important to encourage "The American Drug Cartel" to desire the Republican values that revere God and oppose stealing, assault and slavery methods, which basically force people via threats and violence.

183) It is important to encourage "The American Drug Cartel" to recognize that we are learning to recognize that they are simply dealing medicine products in a crooked Science World connected to Politics, which created the crooked formula that created the Cartels, but that we should know medicine is not actually the Devil nor is it a product that is definitively bad. Medicines are products that can be used with care or carelessly, but they can also be used wrongly by swindlers who trap someone into being intoxicated in their presence so as to steal, swindle, ambush, rape or whatever, but the product in and of itself is not bad, and actually is capable of helping a lot of people through pain and depression among other things.

184) It is important to encourage "The American Drug Cartel" to regulate themselves since there is a political sabotage on them and they are not legally regulated. They need to be encouraged to regulate themselves so as not to price gauge, or to be extortionists but merciful and patient with any debtors, and to be opposed to stealing, assault, lying against neighbors, coveting and everything God's ten commandments tells us along with Christ's reconciliation principles, salvation and to be encouraged to love peace despite American Democrat politics being opposed to private property rights and in favor of Communism slavery.

185) There is one simple option that may actually be ethically viable = Legalize and regulate the current Drug Cartels that are already in place. Why could that be ethically viable? Because crooked politicians and Scientists who corruptly declared medicine as evil and had it outlawed are responsible for having the Cartels be created to deal good medicines illegally when they should have never been illegal in the first place, but rather should have had more medicinal grade forms and potency levels available through regulated legal venues all along.

186) Other sectors of "The American Drug Cartel" that include sex trafficking and gun smuggling should not exist, but could be dealt with from within the Cartel if the Cartels were legalized.

186) Legalizing the current Cartels that are already in place is not a solution that I am proposing without question, but I am analyzing and showing that it may be a viable option.

187) Even consensual sex industry should not be allowed because God's ten commandments oppose adultery and support marriage.

188) The illegal gun smuggling part of the Drug Cartels cannot continue, but I do not know if it is viable or not for them to be licensed and legally keep the same business. It may not be viable to license the Cartel gun smugglers because they may get their resources via other illegal business such as Islamic Terrorist groups overseas, and from stolen guns in America.

189) WHY SHOULDN'T CARTELS BE EDUCATED ABOUT THE BODY, MEDICINE AND NUTRITION? Many and probably most people in the drug culture are not educated, and drug rehabs are not educated either, and religious communities are not educated either, and even the main political conspirators in the Democrat Party and the corrupt Scientists are not

usually educated either in the area of medicinal recovery and good nutrition practices that help a person manage their lives with better appetite balance, which includes balancing their appetites cravings against medicines also not just with foods.

190) If Cartel cultures are more educated about medicine and nutrition, and religious cultures are more educated then they are prone to desire a better balance and being safer with the products they choose as well as being a better influence on one another and not doing as much stereotyping about medicines, which is used to shame and isolate people for the sake of political schemes.

191) Religious communities really don't know very much about medicine, because the extent of what they know is to stereotype people and groups the way the Science community does and the way that media does. Most of what they know is what they are told that one thing is good and one thing is bad, and they don't know much else about it; an example is that they are told coffee is good for you, and they don't really even want to know that it is a dehydrator of the intestines, is acidic, causes withdrawal headaches, makes you lose calcium in your urine, can raise blood pressure, is very acidic, and no one should take a laxative every day. The caffeine in coffee is a medicine just like any other medicine, and has negative side effects.

192) Evolution's lie of multiple races from animals is pure racism.

193) Evolutionists hijacked the top Sciences.

194) Racist Evolutionist's hijacked medicinal Science.

195) Racist Evolutionist's influenced legislators to outlaw the best natural medicines years ago.

196) Racist Evolutionist's are likely suspect for creating the swindler crack cocaine forms dumped in Black communities.

197) When you are dealing with medicines you are dealing with Science, Psychiatry, and Psychology.

198) We need to defund all Evolution venues.

199) We need to be taking Evolution out of Schools.

200) We need Evolutionist's to get out of our medicine making, or to be disqualified from being top decision makers in medicine.

201) We should ban Evolutionist's from running Prisons.

202) We should ban Evolutionist's from the Police department.

203) The KKK had Evolutionist belief's and has no relation to Christianity.

204) The KKK burned crosses in hate of Christ and Christianity.

205) The KKK had a lot to do with prohibition of alcohol and drugs.

206) The KKK influenced religion by demonizing alcohol and drugs.

207) The KKK tricked religions by siding against alcohol and drugs.

208) The KKK's influence from demonizing drugs continues to dominate religious perversion today.

209) The KKK's demonizing of drugs / medicine is what influenced harsh sentencing for non-violent drug offenses.

210) The KKK's demonizing of medicine is what has kept the best medicines illegal and perverted drug rehabilitation.

211) Bottom line is that medicine is a tricky subject and that his how the KKK succeeded in manipulating so many things.

212) Bottom line is that KKK is an Evolutionist group, and Evolution took over the leading Science fields all last Century.

213) KKK is an Evolutionist group and Evolutionists took over Global Warming Science.

214) KKK is an Evolutionist group and Evolutionists coordinated "The American Drug Cartel" via the sabotaging laws.

215) KKK is an Evolutionist group and it is evident they dumped Crack Cocaine on Black populations.

216) KKK is an Evolutionist group and it is evident they coordinated putting Crystal Meth in White populations.

217) What is important to remember about Meth? There are higher class speed forms used to help people work.

218) What is important to remember about Crack? It was designed to steal Black people's money.

219) What should we know about Marijuana? Well, it is somewhat of a sedative, and keeps people at bay.

220) Marijuana is a drug that can cause hallucinations and paranoia in not recognizing things normally.

221) The point about marijuana is that it is not the miracle health drug they claimed it to be mentally.

222) The healthful effects of marijuana are in that it may be helpful to a stressed body, but it still has side effects.

223) Cocaine helps depression and pain, but in strong forms can make people want to do unrealistic things.

224) Cocaine helps depression and pain, but can pop a heart or cause a stroke and should have safer medicine forms.

225) Drug Cartel Scientists know a lot more about medicine and psychology than regular Scientists and Doctors do.

226) Regular Scientists and Doctors are bound to many rules and only get feedback from rats and monkeys.

227) Cartel Scientists get feedback from real human being who choose on their own to be lab rats for medicines.

228) Technically, Americans should have the freedom to be a true Scientist and test their products with cautionary measures.

229) Technically, the freedom to be a Scientist by testing medicines is not a bad thing = It is real Science and should not be outlawed, but should have cautionary standards and measures.

230) Technically, the freedom to be a Scientist being hindered shows how crooked, backward, and how ill-informed our drug laws are.

231) Although, Evolution is fake Science a real Scientist can choose to promote Evolution or hope for it I suppose.

232) Since Evolution is a fake Science then a real Scientist acknowledges that Evolution does not exist that we have ever seen.

233) Technically, a real Scientist cannot believe in Evolution because they have done enough Science tests to see that there is no evidence of Evolution.

234) A real Scientist could play an Evolution game because they favor one Ethnicity over another or just for the money and games to play tricks on people for money or something, a real Scientist knows that we are all part of the same human race and simply have different Ethnicities within humanity.

235) A Medicinal Scientist could believe in Evolution and be racist like that, but may have not studied the Science of humanities origins enough to disprove their own Evolution assumption, and therefore a medicinal Scientists who primarily studies medicinal Science only could indeed be a racist Evolutionist in theory, and could be the type of medicinal Scientist who influenced the outlawing of good medicines, and the type who created the crack cocaine form to dump into Black neighborhoods. Now, the crack cocaine form may not have simply been created to steal money, because it could have been created at first in seeking a quick rush that doesn't last long and lets a person get back to a fairly normal sober fairly quickly - if people can enjoy that approach and not crave more, then that is not such a bad buzz in theory, but there have certainly been designs created so as to make a person crave more after the initial rush.

236) It is also possible that a pure Scientist influenced the drug laws simply for the money, and understood pure Science as created by God but happens to either be a hater of God or simple rejecter of God.

237) It is also possible that a pure Scientist who believed in God influenced making good medicines illegal because they simply believed the risks of pleasurable medicine's overuse were too big of a risk to prescribe or have on the market. That is the believe I have heard from most in the religious communities.

238) I cannot say with 100% certainty whether the original outlawing of good medicine was due to fears of medicinal use or corruption from people

demonizing, but actually when recalling that the KKK demonized medicine - there was a plot behind their stance, so, I believe the demonizing of medicine for the sake of KKK conspiracy came first, and then that led to more rational Scientist, psychologists, and religious people giving into the fears of possible risks in having certain medicines to be legal.

239) I can conclude that the conspiracy to outlaw good medicines was started by the KKK. The KKK is the one who originally demonized various medicines; therefore, the drugophobia ever since, which created all of our irrational laws have been illegitimate fears, and yes, irrational laws.

(reference: Alcohol Problems And Solutions.org; "KKK (Klu Klux Klan), Alcohol & Prohibition: The KKK Supported Prohibition")

240) Technically, what the KKK did in pushing the prohibition was a psychological trick that affected laws and would send people to jail who had an addiction problem or would put people in jail who had a poverty issue and who would sale a medicine for money. My point is that prohibition was not a Science trick at first, but a psychological trick and a psychological trick on the purpose of laws, and that is the same kind of thing that Black racist groups are doing today = They are playing psychological tricks by lying with reverse psychology and calling people that are not racist - racist to appease their own racism and create segregation and potential wars and to put White people out of jobs in favor of contesting racism, which hardly exists and only mostly exists in the form of Black on White racism. There is White on Black racism by White Democrats feeding lies against people who are not racist for the purpose of creating more segregation for Democrats own preferred racist segregation, which also is for helping their Drug Cartel sectors to have more flourishing business and to send Democrat's money.

241) PLUG: Take notice it is not values of Christ causing any of the problems. The values and principles Christ gave us prove to be the solution to all of life's problems. Solutions = Forgiveness, mercy, redemption, treating people fairly, 2nd chances, reverence for God and life, patience, goodness, gentleness, humility, respecting other people's property, respecting other people's right to life, not wanting someone else's property, being married to only one man or woman at a time, not interfering with people's marriage relationships, don't lie about other people, love God, live for Heaven's future more than for being greedy today, be selfish enough to want Heaven and to want to share it, but not greedy, and love + pray for your enemies.

242) I have had push back and been given ultimatums for calling drugs a medicine. So, I write like this sometimes "drug / medicine".

243) Calling a "drug" a medicine is actually the whole point that is missing.

244) A drug is a medicine and a medicine is a drug.

245) Here is the point = We need to view all drugs as medicines.

246) Philosophically, we need to view all medicines as medicine and take a medicine approach.

247) If a medicine approach is taken to drugs, then the instinct is to only use a medicine when you need it, or basically when it lends toward a benefit of relieving a headache, which temporarily helps your memory because headaches temporary inhibit the memory. That is one example showing how a medicine is useful, despite people thinking that a medicine should rarely ever be considered as useful. Well, I agree that the less medicine you depend on the better; but at the same time, it is not a sin and we should not demonize and treat medicine use like the unpardonable sin, even when it is overused or misused in larger doses. Certainly, the cautions of overdose risks should be well known, but the best way for people to learn how to refrain more from medicine is by their own recovery pains, not be being shamed, or forbidden to manage themselves, which often results in a tendency to want to numb the pain of anger, frustration, embarrassment or whatever. People naturally do not like withdrawal symptoms and their best chance of wanting to refrain from medicine is to make it through withdrawal symptoms and to simply not want to have to unnecessarily go through that again, but a difficulty stereotyped people have to deal with is hearing people talk negatively about drug culture stereotypes, which can be typical and bothersome when a person is between 20 and 45, and sometimes their escape from all the negativity is to go visit their drug culture friends, and that might include some drinking or whatever, but it doesn't necessarily have to, and that is where rehab groups actually have some legitimacy, because to get away from the drug free World negativity where people regularly blurt something in anger out about a drug culture stereotype, well, a rehab group is a good get away option over visiting drug culture friends where a relapse has potential.

248) Drug legalization gives drugs a more of a medicinal perception instead of a party perception attraction.

249) Drugs used in parties gives drugs a partying draw, whereas, more

legal forms make drugs a little less attractive in the party scene as drugs are viewed more as a medicine versus for pleasure.

250) It is true that drugs / medicines can bring some pleasurable feelings, but pretty much any drug / medicines side effects are more discomforting than the pleasure features are pleasurable. The pleasurable features of drugs / medicines when used in higher doses usually cause a person to do something out of character that they probably normally would think is either wrong or just not being themselves, and they usually regret their behavior to some degree. Using medicines for any kind of vanity reason is never worth the cost, the embarrassment, the risk, or the withdrawal side effect pains.

251) Essentially, Drug Cartels are simply like Liquor stores being outlawed and continuing to sale their products while gangs form as protection and have look outs for police and people tend to drink together more around the small illegal businesses and that draws in more people both men and women and the domino effect continues on from there. Advanced Cartels include the illegal gun smuggling and illegal sex industry or simply women who regularly ask for money as if everyone is a "Sugar Daddy", which mostly does not involve any sexual relations, but typically becomes a group hangout / getaway. But people who make the money in those circles tend to get greedy about money, because of many reasons including the crowded atmosphere gets on their nerves and periodically the company brings them some descent money, and they begin to expect that more, rather than having to keep the crowd tame and clean up after the crowd. Well, that is one of many ways that things just grow into a hustle type of group.

252) STREET HUSTLERS: Well, when someone is out hustling in the streets all night, drugs / medicines actually help them like a medicine to cope with their fears and to have the energy to be working to make that money. Typically, the Drug Cartels aren't pimping someone and forcing them into the streets, although in some cases, some groups do, or if someone has a debt they owe, but there is typically a trade-off; a person may not have a place to sleep and stays awake all night hustling and wants a medicine to help them. A medicine supplier gives them the medicine if they have money, or if the medicine supplier says the hustler owes them money, they may be out hustling at their own pace when they want to come up with the money, and also in desire of having some medicine sometimes due in part to not having adequate sleep. So, for the most part there is not usually a pimp game going on, the whole thing is about owing money and people wanting medicine - being homeless and a

variety of reasons. Sure, there often appears to be a pimp game but most people out hustling in the streets - both men and women are there by their own choice as I gather. Now, they may have incurred a debt on any given night when they partied too hard and they may be in the streets working to pay off that debt and sometimes debts may be large enough that someone could never pay it off, and that is not fair, but aside from that it appears that most people are willingly doing a street hustle as their own preference. Although, it is their own preference many of them may not feel like they could be hired on a job or that they could not work consistently on time or would not make enough money on a regular minimum wage job, but a felony record may be another thing that causes people to choose a street hustle over trying to find a job and get rejected for their felony record. There can be many reasons. So, although street hustling is a close proximity preference by many in the drug cultures - that does not mean it is their first preference, I am just saying that in most cases they are not forced out there, but Cartels are not regulated so there are also many groups that may actually force a person into the hustle or simply be threatening them if they don't get money "right now!" and their best quick money option in that case is usually a street hustle and not a preference in that case, but is a close proximity preference - the only other good option is to find a bus ticket to another City.

253) CASES WHERE STREET HUSTLERS ARE FORCED TO HUSTLE: Well, although, I think more are not forced than are forced - there is no regulation, so there is nothing stopping someone from forcing street hustlers to hustle, except for people in their circles if they have family values or some neighborly values from God. IF SOMEONE IS BEING FORCED then it is not like a regular job where they can go to the Police or anyone and ask for help. Some Police would tell them "well, what do you expect - if you are hanging around drugs and drug gangs - that is the kind of thing you get". Others would tell them that unfortunately we cannot do anything about it because you are involved in illegal activity. NOTE: I think Police are wrong to say that and not protect someone from being forced to work the streets like a slave, and to not protect someone from threats of violence. However, who is safe to ask the Police for help in that situation in the first place? If the bully found out that the street hustler told Police that he is forcing them to work the street, and the Police do not immediately detain that bully, then the street hustler is in much bigger trouble with the bully than they were in the first place. BASICALLY, this ends up revealing another point in favor of legalizing street medicines for the sake of thorough regulation.

254) Are the drug laws so important that we should continue to have a

segregated nation within a nation while the lawful nation is declared to be under God and the Drug Cartel nation is declared as not worthy of God?

255) A nation without God is a nation without love. The supposed lawful side of the nation under God is not loving the Drug Cartel nation, but rather has defined them as unpardonable to God and man, and that is a heresy, which is NOT of God.

256) When I say the supposed lawful side of the nation in #255 - I say it in the context of them having agreed with Democrats in making some crooked laws that they follow and have declared those who don't follow it as unlawful, but the law itself is impractical and was set up for corrupt reasons way back during the prohibition, which the conspiring KKK was a leader in.

257) One of the biggest problems with "The American Drug Cartel" is that many and possibly most religious Christian sectors worship "The Ten Commandments Of Evolution" instead of "The Ten Commandments Of God".

258) Many or most religious Christian communities have trusted Scientists to be knowledgeable beyond average human knowledge and have had a double standard in partly accepting Evolution based on what Scientist's say, although, when addressed directly about what the Bible say's about origins the religious person will acknowledge they agree with the Bible also, which defies Evolution and claims + shows we all came from Adam and Eve. In one classroom religious people agree with the Bible, but at the Hospital and among Scientists many religious people will agree with a false Scientist while assuming Scientists know more than other people.

259) Scientist's lie just like anyone else can.

260) Many Scientists are students of other Scientist's, and simply trust their teachers whether they are lying or not.

261) Doctors are basically students of Scientist's.

262) Doctors are often either deluded, shortsighted, or lying when they promote coffee.

263) Many Doctor's claim coffee is healthy simply because they are addicted to it themselves.

264) Coffee is like any medicine but worse in various ways.

265) Coffee has multiple negative side effects; it is healthier to take a caffeine supplement than to drink coffee regularly.

266) Like any medicine - it is okay to drink coffee for one or two days for some specific reason, but one should break the addiction ASAP after one or two days of using. I suggest only using coffee 1 day as part of a cleanse, and no more than 1 day.

267) Why is coffee more potent than other medicines? Coffee has more features than a simple pill medicine or a singular medicine. The features in coffee are not bad when used as a medicine for one day or two days at the most, except that you will still have side effects, but coffee is a laxative + diuretic + adrenal gland initiator + has acid that picks up your body temperature + has caffeine.

   The problem with diuretics and laxatives is that they dehydrate your kidneys and intestines and body, but the advantage to those things is that it can be considered a cleanse - the disadvantage is in dehydrating and cleansing two days in a row taking a toll on the body. The disadvantage of using a laxative daily is very bad, because as many say "life is in the intestines", well you don't want your intestines to stay dehydrated - intestines are the most important body part for a majority of functions to stay hydrated regularly; hydration is important full circle - your kidneys and liver need to stay hydrated and so does your integumentary system, but your intestines simply perform a few extra duties that we don't often think about.

   It is not good to regularly induce your adrenal gland function and to wear out your adrenal glands.

   It is not good to regularly depend on caffeine for brain energy, which only works part of the brain and it is not good to have a headache with memory challenges when withdrawing from caffeine. Caffeine affects temperament and lends toward a short tension span.

268) Caffeine is helpful to people's awake energy who have schedules that cause them to lack enough sleep.

269) True Christianity offers the solutions beyond misconceptions in this World.

270) No matter how delusional this World is - Christ's forgiveness and reconciliation principles always have a benefit.

271) No matter how delusional I may be in a situation - Christ's values are still applicable and helpful.

272) This book tells you there is an "American Drug Cartel" not just a "Mexican Drug Cartel". I tell you a little about "The American Drug Cartel" and the political formulas and lies about medicine that created it and keep it running. I tell you about ways to help people and understand their situation if they dealing with psychological fears, traps, and addictions from the drug culture. I tell you ways to work toward promoting peace and less violence in society and in "The American Drug Cartel", I give you perspectives on Cartels in general, which can help have a better perspective with "The Mexico Drug Cartel" also = They simply a medicine based pharmacy to simplify, but laws complicate and they expand into gun smuggling and sex industry similar to any illegal medicine dealing groups who develop a network of protection and have a medicine party approach more so than a medicine health approach.

   I will do more to explain Christian principles and God's laws of governing in a few other chapters in this book, because Christian principles represent the solutions to more neighborly living cross culturally, and are applicable universally to any solution-oriented book, discussion, governing system, classroom, business, family, or network.

273) Always remember when dealing with philosophy that we are always dealing with human beings no matter if they are violent or are part of a group known for violence. Yes, extreme measures have to be used in extreme situations, but anytime there is a forum where good values, peace and patience can be inserted, we must remember that everyone is human and is a neighbor who needs to know their rightful freedom is the right to life, respect for their property, and they have a right to have knowledge of God and His neighbor loving commands, and a right to be able to discuss and understand truth over lies.

274) Know that top Scientists are capable of making any medicine, which includes the current pain medicines used after surgery, such as "Lortab" (Hydrocodone) – lesser addictive, and lower potency. Scientists are capable of making street medicines safer just like any other medicine, and the corrupt Science being run by anti-human dignity Evolutionist's have made many rules that Demonize good Scientists who would attempt to make better medicines. In other word's the Corrupt Politician's, legislator's,

and Scientist's mostly connected to the American Democrat Party have put so many corrupt laws in place that it is blocking good Scientist's from having the freedom to make a safer medicine World while simultaneously demonizing other medicines. I can think of one clear example where a natural sleeping pill that comes directly from protein in food called L-Tryptophan was outlawed back in 1982 as I recall, but I searched the internet and found permanent bans in 1989 and 1990 by the FDA. I recall it finally being legal again around 2006 or so. It went back on the market and came back off the market again in many places, because the corrupt Science community has continued contesting it? Why do I think they contest that? Because, it takes business away from their chemically based new experimental sleep medicines they create, and those are clearly not the healthy option. Since I have studied nutrition a lot on my own and experimented with healthy supplements and diets; I can also tell you that the FDA has tried to ban natural herbal remedies and other healthy items in your health stores, because the FDA does not get money from those natural products like they do from medicines that have their stamp of approval on it. So, the corruption is for many reasons, but also to support the FDA drug sales versus supporting the healthiest options.

275) The example above in #274 clearly proves my case in this book about the corrupt formulas of politicians, legislators, and the corrupt side of the Science community in having created the Drug Cartels pathway and an underground society filled with assault, slavery, and theft.

Chapter 2 = Bible Verses For The Heart, Soul, And Mind

Romans 10:9 'That if thou shalt confess with thy mouth that Jesus is Lord, and shalt believe in thine heart that God hath raised him from the dead, thou shalt be saved.'

John 3:17 'For God sent not His Son into the world to condemn the world, but that the world through Him might be saved.'

Proverbs 9:10 "The fear of the Lord is the beginning of wisdom: and the knowledge of the holy is understanding."

Matthew 6:9-13 is "The Lord's Prayer", that He taught for His followers.

John 4:24 "God is a Spirit: and they that worship Him must worship Him in

Spirit and in Truth."

John 10:30 "I and my Father are one."

John 14:6 "Jesus said unto him, I am the way, the truth, and the life: no man cometh unto the Father, but by me."

1 John 4:8 'He that loves not, knows not God, for God is love.'

Luke 6:31 (Christ's Golden Rule) "And as ye would that men should do to you, do ye also to them likewise."

Luke 6:27-28 'Love your enemies, do good to those who hate you, bless those who curse you, pray for those who mistreat you'.

John 3:16 'For God so loved the world that He gave His only begotten Son, that whosoever believeth in Him should not perish but have everlasting life.'

Romans 12:1-2 'I beseech you therefore, brethren, by the mercies of God, that ye present your bodies a living sacrifice, holy acceptable unto God, which is your reasonable service. And be not conformed to this world: but be ye transformed by the renewing of your mind, that ye may prove what is that good, and acceptable, and perfect, will of God.'

Hebrews 11:6 "But without faith it is impossible to please Him: for he that cometh to God must believe that He is, and that He is a rewarder of them that diligently seek Him."

Hebrews 12:1,2 "Wherefore seeing we are also compassed about with so great a cloud of witnesses, let us lay aside every weight, and the sin which doth so easily beset us, and let us run with patience the race that is set before us, 2 Looking to Jesus the Author and finisher of our faith; who for the joy that was set before Him endured the cross, despising the shame, and is set down at the right hand of the throne of God."

2 Timothy 2:15 'Study to show thyself approved unto God, a workman that needed not to be ashamed, rightly dividing the Word of truth.'

2 Timothy 1:7 'For God has not given us a Spirit of fear, but of power, and of love and of a sound mind.'

Galatians 5:22-23 'But the fruit of the Spirit is love, joy, peace, longsuffering, gentleness, goodness, faith, meekness, temperance: against such there is no law.'

Matthew 22:36-40 'Master, which is the great commandment in the law? Jesus said unto him, Thou shalt love the Lord thy God with all thy heart, and with all thy soul, and with all thy mind. This is the first and great commandment. And the second is like unto it, Thou shalt love thy neighbor as thyself. On these two commandments hang all the law and the prophets.

Exodus 20 lists 'The Ten Commandments' which are 10 simple commandments from God for governing private life, and society with. (Thou shalt not steal, kill, covet, bear false witness against thy neighbor, nor shalt thou commit adultery, nor have any other gods before me, Honor thy father and mother that you days may be long on the earth, Remember the sabbath day, to keep it holy...)

Proverbs 31:4-7 "It is not for kings, O Lemuel, it is not for kings to drink wine; nor for princes strong drink: 5 Lest they drink, and forget the law, and pervert the judgement of any of the afflicted.

6 Give strong drink unto him that is ready to perish, and wine unto those that be heavy of hearts. 7 Let him drink, and forget his poverty, and remember his misery no more."

1 John 1:8 'If we say that we have no sin, we deceive ourselves, and the truth is not in us.'

1 John 1:9 'But if we confess our sins, God is faithful and just to forgive us our sins, and to cleanse us from all unrighteousness.'

James 1:5-6 'If any of you lack wisdom, let him ask of God, that giveth to all men liberally, and upbraideth not; and it shall be given him. But let him ask in faith, nothing wavering. For he that wavereth is like a wave of the sea driven with the wind and tossed.'

Psalm 1 'Blessed is the man who walketh not in the counsel of the ungodly, nor standeth in the way with sinners, nor sitteth in the seat of the scornful, but his delight is in the law of the Lord, and in this law doth he meditate day and night. And he shall be like the tree planted by the rivers of water who bringeth forth his fruit in his season; his leaf also shall not whither; and whatsoever he doeth shall prosper. The ungodly are not so: but are like the chaff which the wind driveth away. Therefore the ungodly shall not stand in the judgement, nor sinners in the congregation of the righteous. For the Lord knoweth the way of the righteous: but the way of the ungodly shall perish.'

Ephesians 4:30-32 " And grieve not the Spirit of God, whereby ye are sealed unto the day of redemption. Let all bitterness, and wrath, and anger, and clamour, and evil speaking, be put away from you, with all malice: And be ye kind one to another, tenderhearted, forgiving one another, even as God for Christ's sake hath forgiven you."

2 Chronicles 7:14 "If my people who are called by my name, will humble themselves and pray, and seek my face, and turn from their wicked ways, then will I hear from Heaven, and will forgive their sins, and will heal their land."

Romans 1:16 "For I am not ashamed of the gospel of Christ: for it is the power of God unto salvation to every one that believeth; to the Jew first, and also to the Greek."

Romans 8:28 "And we know that all things work together for good to them that love God, to them who are the called according to His purpose."

1 Peter 5:8 "Be sober, be vigilant; because your adversary the devil, as a roaring lion, walketh about, seeking whom he may devour:"

GOD IS VERY MERCIFUL, BUT REPENTANCE TIME RUNS OUT:

Genesis 18:26 "And the Lord said, If I find in Sodom fifty righteous within the city, then I will spare all the place for their sakes."

Genesis 18:32 "And he (Abraham) said, Oh let not the Lord be angry, and I will speak yet but this once: Peradventure ten (righteous) shall be found there. And he (the Lord) said, I will not destroy it for ten's sake."

Genesis 19:24-25 "Then the Lord rained upon Sodom and upon Gomorrah brimstone and fire from the Lord out of heaven; And he overthrew those cities, and all the plain, and all the inhabitants of the cities, and that which grew upon the ground."

THE WORLDWIDE FLOOD OF NOAH'S TIME:

Genesis 7:19-24

19 And the waters prevailed exceedingly upon the earth; and all the high hills, that were under the whole heaven, were covered.
20 Fifteen cubits upward did the waters prevail; and the mountains were covered.
21 And all flesh died that moved upon the earth, both of fowl, and of cattle, and of beast, and of every creeping thing that creepeth upon the earth, and every man:
22 All in whose nostrils was the breath of life, of all that was in the dry land, died.
23 And every living substance was destroyed which was upon the face of the ground, both man, and cattle, and the creeping things, and the fowl of the heaven; and they were destroyed from the earth: and Noah only remained alive, and they that were with him in the ark.
24 And the waters prevailed upon the earth an hundred and fifty days.

GOD'S PROMISE AFTER THE FLOOD:
Genesis 8:22 "While the earth remaineth, seedtime and harvest, and cold and heat, and summer and winter, and day and night shall not cease.

Genesis 9:11-13
11 And I will establish my covenant with you, neither shall all flesh be cut off any more by the waters of a flood; neither shall there anymore be a flood to destroy the earth.

12 And God said, This is the token of the covenant

which I make between me and you and every living creature that is with you, for perpetual generations:
13 I do set my bow in the cloud, and it shall be for a token of a covenant between me and the earth.
ONE HUMAN RACE CAME FROM NOAH'S FAMILY AFTER THE FLOOD:

Genesis 9:18-19

18 And the sons of Noah, that went forth of the ark, were Shem, and Ham, and Japheth: and Ham is the father of Canaan.
19 These are the three sons of Noah: and of them was the whole earth overspread.

Genesis 9:6 Whoso sheddeth man's blood, by man shall his blood be shed: for in the image of God made he man.

THE TEN COMMANDMENTS: (Exodus 20:1-22)

1 **And God spoke all these words, saying,**
2 I am the Lord thy God, which have brought thee out of the land of Egypt, out of the house of bondage.
3 Thou shalt have no other gods before me.
4 Thou shalt not make unto thee any graven image, or any likeness of any thing that is in heaven above, or that is in the earth beneath, or that is in the water under the earth.
5 Thou shalt not bow down thyself to them, nor serve them: for I the Lord thy God am a jealous God, visiting the iniquity of the fathers upon the children unto the third and fourth generation of them that hate me;
6 And shewing mercy unto thousands of them that

love me, and keep my commandments.

7 Thou shalt not take the name of the Lord thy God in vain; for the Lord will not hold him guiltless that taketh his name in vain.

8 Remember the sabbath day, to keep it holy.

9 Six days shalt thou labor, and do all thy work:

10 But the seventh day is the sabbath of the Lord thy God: in it thou shalt not do any work, thou, nor thy son, nor thy daughter, thy manservant, nor thy maidservant, nor thy cattle, nor thy stranger that is within thy gates:

11 For in six days the Lord made heaven and earth, the sea, and all that in them is, and rested the seventh day: wherefore the Lord blessed the sabbath day, and hallowed it.

12 Honour thy father and thy mother: that thy days may be long upon the land which the Lordthy God giveth thee.

13 Thou shalt not kill.

14 Thou shalt not commit adultery.

15 Thou shalt not steal.

16 Thou shalt not bear false witness against thy neighbour.

17 Thou shalt not covet thy neighbour's house, thou shalt not covet thy neighbour's wife, nor his manservant, nor his maidservant, nor his ox, nor his ass, nor any thing that is thy neighbour's.

18 And all the people saw the thunderings, and the lightnings, and the noise of the trumpet, and the mountain smoking: and when the people saw it, they removed, and stood afar off.

19 And they said unto Moses, Speak thou with us, and we will hear: but let not God speak with us, lest we

die.

20 And Moses said unto the people, Fear not: for God is come to prove you, and that his fear may be before your faces, that ye sin not.

21 And the people stood afar off, and Moses drew near unto the thick darkness where God was.

22 And the Lord said unto Moses, Thus thou shalt say unto the children of Israel, Ye have seen that I have talked with you from heaven.

Proverbs 23 Warns against gluttony and drunkenness.

Proverbs 31 Speaks about medicinal drinking in the first part of the chapter, and speaks about the virtuous woman in the second part of the chapter.

Ecclesiastes 1 = Vanity of vanities all is vanity.

Ecclesiastes 7 has lessons on wisdom.

Ecclesiastes 12 = Life is short, keep God's commandments.

Matthew 5-7 = Christ's famous "Sermon On The Mount". Christ speak on many good things in chapter 5 including on the ten commandments. Matthew 6 includes "The Lord's Prayer".

Luke 6 = Christ's "Golden Rule" and "love your enemies".

John 8:1-11 = Pharisees bring Jesus a woman caught in adultery, and Jesus responds.

John 10 = Christ is the door of the sheep, and Christ say's "I and the Father are One".

John 14 = Christ says, "I am in the Father and the Father in me."

Romans 3 shows that Jews and Gentiles have equal reconciliation.

Romans 10 is Paul praying and imploring Jews to receive Christ's salvation.

Romans 12 says to "be transformed by the renewing of your mind."

1 Corinthians 7 = Paul talks about marriage and being single.

1 Corinthians 13 = Paul defines Godly love.

1 Corinthians 14 = Paul shows that teaching over speaking in tongues is most important.

1 Corinthians 15 = Paul teaches the importance of resurrection.

In Galatians 6 = Paul talks about "bearing one another's burdens".

Ephesians 5 = Paul talks about redeeming time, and departing from evil.

Ephesians 6 = Put on the armor of God.

Colossian 1 = Christ is God.

Colossians 2 = Let no man judge you by holy days but in Christ.

Colossians 3 = Set your affections above, be merciful, and kind...

2 Timothy 1 = Have a sound mind, do not be ashamed, endure:

2 Timothy 2 = Study, and avoid vain babbling for others sake:

Hebrews 11 talks about faith as an utmost necessity.

Hebrews 12 = God chastens His children, educe the race.

James 1 = Be ye doers of the word, and talks about enduring temptation.

James 2 = Faith without works is dead - respect people equally.

James 3 = Warnings about the tongue.

James 4 = Draw nigh to God, resist the Devil, and He will flee from you.

James 5 = Be patient unto the coming of the Lord.

1 John 1 includes, "If we say we have no sin, God's truth is not in us."

1 John 2 = Love not the World, Hate not your brother.

1 John 3 = Love in deed and in truth.

1 John 4 = God is love and we ought to love also.

1 John 5 = Keeping God's commandments is not grievous if we love God.

Revelation 20:10 "And the devil that deceived them was cast into the lake of fire and brimstone, where the beast and the false prophet are, and shall be tormented day and night for ever and ever."

Hell is not a deception = It is for deceivers. Reality Harmonizer Bob

Chapter 3 = Better World Keys

1) The Republican USA embraced this Master Key = Revere being under the only evidenced God who created us all equally Human in His image.

2) "Love your neighbor" with private property rights which include yourself, your money, family, land, house, apartment, cars, miscellaneous items, bank accounts, stock benefits, insurance, 401K, your Business, your ID, your Diplomas, your Animals...

3) "Love your neighbor" with God's "10 commandments".

4) "Love your neighbor" with strong National border security, and that is for your neighboring Nation across the border as well as your own. When you have weak borders and are inviting violence and thievery into your Nation then you are inviting violence and thievery to cross into and through your neighboring Nation also, and you are a bad neighbor if you are doing that.

5) "Love your neighbor" with "thou shalt not murder" held in high value.

6) "Love your neighbor" with low tax rates that respect private property rights, and are so low that the rates cannot be considered as stealing or

swindling citizens.

7) "Love your neighbor" with respect for independence under God the Creator.

8) "Love your neighbor" with respect for independence for all Nations and respect for their people's safety starting at their borders, and with rebuke against any contrary deception for border security.

9) "Love your neighbor" with the "Freedom Of Religion" and the outlawing of "False Religious Cults".

10) "Love your neighbor" with the "Freedom Of Speech" to pursue truth over lies, education about true Religion which has evidence of God for a second life, and freedom to speak about Politics and needs...

11) "Love your neighbor" with laws against "false accusations against people".

12) "Love your neighbor" with laws that expect reverence of God and His commandments in Police enforcement, and with laws that guard against having too many laws, and against having petty laws.

13) "Love your neighbor" with "thou shalt not steal, lie, cheat, swindle or covet". ("Mind your own business")

14) "Love your neighbor" with natural family and parenting laws that revere "thou shalt not commit adultery" with adulterous and dishonest laws or in relationships.

15) "Love your neighbor" with natural family and natural parenting laws that highly value the lives of children as neighbors created in the image of God, and that highly value bringing a child into the World in loving relationships by natural Parents, and values a woman's womb as sacred.

16) "Love your neighbor" with a good stewardship Business system where neighbors Humanely work together, are rewarded for their labor in a system that recognizes God and His redeeming principles for Humanity with orderliness that competes for a job, but does not compete to be viewed as a machine, but rather as a co-laboring neighbor for wise survival and success under God.

17) "Love your neighbors and enemies" with a good "Reconciliation

System" under God that does not allow for cults to be exercised in the "Reconciliation System". Work toward having Humane quarters and treatment of people. It should be a place to learn good peacemaking skills and a peaceful oriented place with dignity, and facility's designed to lend to dignity in the bathing and restroom process. "All have sinned and come short of the glory of God." Romans 3:23. Christ commands us to forgive everyone and seek neighborly justice and redemption, not revenge, and to treat others the way we would want to be treated when caught in a fault.

18) "Love your neighbors and enemies" with a renewing Godly "Justice System". Remembering God in the "Justice System" is of utmost importance. Christ's Golden rule of "Do to others as you would have them do to you." - Has a high usage propensity value within the "Justice System". We cannot forget one of the great things about the USA in coming up with "innocent until proven guilty". Better World seeking Nations should continue to insert more of Christ's principles in Justice, and understand that forgiveness is always necessary, and that forgiveness does NOT mean pardon - it means to seek neighborly Godly justice instead of revenge, and although, pardon is an option, a level of mercy is always good and expected because God is merciful, and we are only Human and are therefore imperfect Judges, so, we therefore, should always observe a level of mercy while being cognizant of "an eye for an eye", and consider the safety of the Public in how sentencing is assessed. Remember this simple principle = "Over punishing is stealing." Assessing the repentant and unrepentant is not very important in cases of non-violence because we cannot see the heart, only God can, but trying to assess the repentant and unrepentant in violent cases has relevance to the small degree that it is possible - In either case a person can pay their debt in a non-violent crime and be returned to society with the counsel of living a neighborly and repentant life under God, but a person who committed a violent crime depending on the severity and circumstances should not be released early if there is a questionable violent behavior pattern via mental issues or apparent unrepentance, there can be work-release options, mental institution options, or detainment facilities hat are more residential with working options, or if extreme violence is continually pursued while in the "Reconciliation System" the death penalty may quickly become the best and appropriate option, because they cannot be assumed peaceful to society, and they cannot ruin the peace and safety within the "Reconciliation Detainment Facility" either. The system should be very careful not to overcharge anyone financially, or in time served, nor shorten time served which could be unsafe to the Public via payouts and bailouts. The system should not be influenced by money, but rather by careful,

neighborly and Godly discernment. A person should not pay more than seven times the amount of a stolen item, and pardon is also an option the victim has authority to choose unless it is deemed that they need the courts protected decision.

19) We live in a modernized medicine World, but we have much crooked Science, and false Evolution in the recent last Century who demonized medicines, and influenced the Creation of predatory medicine laws, and the demonizing and over punishing of medicinal consumers. Society's need to expect better medicines from Scientists including better legal forms of street medicines. Many street medicines are designed into swindler forms, and do not have to be, Scientists can pull out the anti-depressant and pain-relieving features in many street medicines while leaving out the more addictive features, and they can make lower potency and longer lasting forms that are safer, and that do not create the withdrawal symptoms of short lasting, high potency swindler forms. THE LAWS SHOULD BE TARGETED AT MEDICINAL PROVIDERS AND STREET DEALERS, but they should not be demonized but rather judged individually as to whether they are violent or non-violent, howbeit, with the acknowledged risk of receiving and selling unlabeled and unregulated product (over punishing is stealing and winds up favoring violent mobs who protect the violent dealing sectors - assess case by case with mercy to create an employment advocating society). The consumers should simply be expected to use at their own risk, and be held responsible for their behavior when they are intoxicated, and be sent to rehabs that do not interfere with their jobs or reputations under new regulation laws. Enforcement should deal with stealing and violence the same as they would if no medicine were involved, and the issues with illegal dealing should be clearly understood rather than demonized so-as to protect people from price gauging, medicinal inconsistency, tax evading, regulation for poisoning and risk of not knowing what all is in the product, being required to label the ingredients, extortion - - While much of the problems can be solved by CROOKED Science being called out and creating safer legal forms of all medicines. Nutritional and Exercise venues for Health should become popular so consumers learn to understand how the body best operates, and that Physical nutrition and exercise is the best deterrence from relying on medicinal crutches and to gain a Healthy disdain for living with medicinal side effects. The protection of "thou shalt not steal" should apply equally for medicinal consumers as it does for non-medicinal consumers. "Love your neighbor as yourself."

20) "Love God and your neighbor" by seeking to have a GOOD Nation, and by sharing your successful methods and hope in God with other

Nations and all people around the World. Why let a God hating portion in your Nation demand that you cannot share all the good that you know with all of God's creation locally and Globally under the auspice of being loving neighbors "under God", and for the sake of living in peace, and to live enjoying what little wealth you have and affording the same for others through sharing the well-known wise philosophy for tangible, realistic prosperous and sustainable living "under God".

21) A better World only comes from God-Christ's-Spirit.

22) Jesus Christ = Pure Love = Sovereign God.

23) God-Christ's-Spirit commands us to make a better World = "Love God with all your heart, soul and mind & Love your neighbor as yourself".

24) Making a better World is actually very simple = Everyone just needs to love their neighbors under God, and if they do, then we have the best possible World - WELL, although, knowing how to make a better World is very clear, not all People, and sometimes not even many People will love their neighbors like they should. Some People live for hate of life, hate of God and for hating other People, BUT we can certainly teach the key command of God to "love our neighbors and enemies" - we can show forgiveness and redemption, and many People are bound to choose the safe Ship in Christ and living for a better World.

25) I want a better World from, for, in, thru, and with God-Christ's-Spirit now, and in Heaven where we get the best World.

26) We should all want a better World as God-Christ's-Spirit commands us to make.

27) There is no doubt that living in a World where there is no violence or stealing would be a much better World, and that is the kind of World that God's "10 Commandments" tells us to work for, and to live by.

28) Be neighborly, beyond Earth's norms.

29) True neighborliness does not require money; it requires sharing wisdom and pursuing Godly justice for People.

30) We do not have to feel faith in resurrected Christ as God - We trust in Christ as God, and we HAVE faith in Christ as God. Faith is a choice. "CHOOSE you this day whom you will serve" (Joshua 24:15).

A believer feels comfort in trusting and having faith in Christ for eternity, because they genuinely trust in the second life of eternal peace that Christ offers, and because He gives believers His Holy Spirit of love, joy, peace, patience, temperance, goodness, meekness, gentleness, faith to walk with in daily repentance, and hope. God-Christ's-Spirit does comfort us, but we often have to figure out if our mind is telling us something or if God is telling us something. Usually, in proper, a believer's mind is discerning what God wants, and His will of evangelizing is laid out clearly in the Bible, and we can do His will in whatever vocation we choose or wherever we live.

Chapter 4 = Things To Pray For Repetitiously

1) Regularly ask God for wisdom in all facets + all specific facets that you can think of - God always grants in the affirmative for this request.

James 1:5 "If any of you lack wisdom, let him ask of God, that giveth to all men liberally, and upbraideth not; and it shall be given him."

2) Psalm 51:10-13 "Create in me a clean heart, O God; and renew a right spirit within me. Cast me not away from thy presence; and take not thy holy spirit from me. Restore unto me the joy of thy salvation; and uphold me with thy free spirit."

3) Pray before bed that the Holy Spirit will intercede for you all during your sleep, and pray again in the morning and anytime you remember to that the Holy Spirit will intercede for you all day to pray in you 'without ceasing' for direction, understanding, answers, peace...

Romans 8:26 "Likewise the Spirit also helpeth our infirmities: for we know not what we should pray for as we ought: but the Spirit itself maketh intercession for us with groaning which cannot be uttered."

4) Pray, "Lord, help me, help me, help me..."

Psalm 5:1-2 "Give ear to my words, O Lord, consider my meditation. Hearken unto the voice of my cry, my King, and my God: for unto thee will I pray."

5) Ask God for forgiveness of sins regularly including sins of apathetic attitude among other things =

1 John 1:9-10 says, 9) "If we confess our sins, He is faithful and just to forgive us our sins and to cleanse us from all unrighteousness.
10) If we say that we have not sinned, we make Him a liar, and His word is not in us."

6) Pray Psalm 23 in a requesting way = "Lord, lead me into green pastures, restore my soul, lead me in the paths of righteousness for Thy names sake. Give me confidence in the valley of the shadow of death. Comfort me with Thy rod and Thy staff. Prepare a table before me in the presence of mine enemies. Anoint my head with oil, fill my cup Lord. Lord, I ask for awareness of your goodness and mercy all of the days of my life, for I know with Christ as my Lord that I shall dwell in the house of the Lord forever.

7) Pray for understanding when you read Scripture.

8) Pray for help in applying Scripture when you walk away from meditation and study on Scripture.

9) Pray for protection against the ungodly and that you will not partake in mocking or scorning publicly or in your mind or heart, and that you recognize the difference and what is good, such as encouragement, gentleness, goodness, mercy, grace, forgiveness...

10) Pray for endurance, energy, stamina, and emotional interest to meditate on God's laws day and night. (Psalm 1)

11)

Make Me an Instrument of Your Peace

Lord, make me an instrument of your peace.
Where there is hatred, let me sow love,

Where there is injury, pardon
Where there is doubt, faith,
Where there is despair, hope,
Where there is darkness, light,
Where there is sadness, joy.
O Divine Master, grant that I may not so much
seek to be consoled as to console,
not so much to be understood as to understand,
not so much to be loved, as to love;
for it is in giving that we receive,
it is in pardoning that we are pardoned,
it is in dying that we awake to eternal life.

--- St. Francis of Assisi

12) "The Lord's Prayer" summarization from Matthew 6:9-13 = Praise God in Heaven, Ask for His will to be done, His Kingdom to be emulated on earth through you and those around you and systems around you, ask for food both spiritual and physical, ask for forgiveness of trespasses, and ask God to deliver you from evil, and praise God for His Kingdom and power and glory that is forever...

13) Pray for more peace awareness in your heart, and temperance in difficult times.

14) Pray for a proper meek and humble perspective under God and not the often-taught superficial humility that ignores truth.

15) Pray for discernment in justice, mercy, grace, redemption and reconciliation for yourself and rightful measures for various offenders.

16) Pray from the list above and the list below for both your neighbors and enemies, but for protection against enmity.

17) Pray for God to fill gaps of loneliness with more Holy Spirit and His fruit + truth, recognition of common Spirit agenda's, and wisdom in choosing acquaintances and sometimes friends who compliment the will of God.

18) A reworded paraphrase of a key point in Reinhold Niebuhr's "Serenity Prayer" = "Change what you can, don't worry or waste time with what you

can't, and prayer for wisdom to know the difference."

19) Psalm 119:37 "Turn away mine eyes from beholding vanity; and quicken thou me in thy way."

20) Psalm 119:33 "Teach me, O Lord, the way of Thy statutes..."

21) 1 Thessalonians 5:18 "In everything give thanks: for this is the will of God in Christ Jesus concerning you."

22) Pray that God gives you a recognition of His holy love, grace and compassion to share, and regular communion with His Holy Spirit.

23) Ask for increased faith as you do the works of faith. (Luke 17)

24) Ask God to give you songs of faith and encouragement to bring to your memory as needed for His praise and for you to walk in the Spirit.

25) Ask God to give you proper contentment in every situation, and to have discernment for redeeming the time for Heavenly investments.

26) Ask God to arm you with His whole Armor that Paul talks about in Ephesians 6.

27) Ephesians 6:18 "Praying always with all prayer and supplication in the Spirit, and watching thereunto with all perseverance and supplication for all saints;"

28) In Ephesians 6:19-20 Paul ask for Christians to pray for him "that utterance may be given unto me, that I may open my mouth boldly, to make known the mystery of the gospel, 20 For which I am an ambassador in bonds: that therein I may speak boldly, as I ought to speak." = Pray for your CHRISTIAN SPEAKERS regularly, and CHRISTIANS FRIENDS and Christian acquaintances regularly to know how to speak and minister in whatever they do...

29) Ask God for self-control in food appetite and other things and wisdom in managing appetites.

30) Ask God for miracle salvation revivals all over the world, in your city, State, Country, Church, schools, other Churches, in media, among politicians, in poor society's, in wealthy society's...

31) Ask God for "under God" reverence, discernment, wisdom and knowledge revivals in governments, politics, justice system, reconciliation system, legislation, churches...

32) Pray for your political leaders both friends and enemies. Pray all of the above points on this list for them (minus blessing enemies with resources to destroy you - pray for change of heart, the spiritual things...), and for wisdom and guidance in their job, and repentance where needed.

33) Pray for God to help you be single minded throughout life, ask God to purify your heart toward being single minded versus double minded. Derived from James 1:8 = "A double minded man is unstable in all his ways."

34) One thing that God gave to Jesus was increased strength after Jesus prayed to let the cup of crucifixion pass from Him if possible. Jesus was not like us and did not have to ask for wisdom regularly the same way we do, but when Jesus prayed that prayer before His crucifixion, God granted Him increased strength, SO, MY POINT IS ONE I LEFT OUT UNTIL NOW = ASK GOD FOR INCREASED ENDURANCE STRENGTH, STRENGTH IN PATIENCE AND WHATEVER STRENGTH HE WILL INCREASE DURING HARD TIMES...

35) PRAYER FOR HUMILITY: (A prayer and a lesson in studied prayer points to pray regularly generated from pondered times where I know pride can creep in in my own path's)
Lord, I pray for humility, and the rightful discerning of it when I am eating, sleeping, communicating, thinking, drinking, walking, talking, stressed, defending myself in various degrees, and pray I am humble enough to stand up for myself when I should, and that I discern the humility to know when it is not necessary to engage in defense, but to just be silent, or give a soft answer, and help me to be humble in my positions with God as a human being, as a child of God, as a believer in Christ as Lord of all, as a servant of God, as a teacher in sharing of insights I learn from meditating on and discerning truth based on Biblical principles, and as I claim confidence in some knowledge, and remind me to be humble to remember that I still do not know very much compared to the knowledge that exists in God's universe. I pray for humility in so many areas = in every area that is visible and not visible to me when each situation arises, such as the humility I need when I am enjoying or working along with the emphasis of each fruit of the Spirit = Humility in love, Humility in joy, Humility in peace,

Humility in patience, Humility in gentleness, Humility in goodness, Humility in Faith, Humility in hope, Humility in temperance, Humility in forgiveness, Humility in understanding, Humility in wisdom, Humility in truth pursuit, Humility in worship, Humility in heart, soul, spirit, and mind, and Humility in stress, and Humility for repentance when angry, and Humility in times of righteous anger...May the Humility addressed always be the kind of Humility that Christ teaches, and when Humbleness is addressed that it is not addressed as in a way to puff up pride, although, it may be discussed as a topic of reality or self-defense in describing a pursuit of humility being engaged in, though, one cannot rightly or perfectly grade their own humility or anyone else, and only God can grade one's understanding and practice level in various aspects of humility applied in one's life precisely, BUT thank you for grace, mercy, and forgiveness, and may I remember to be humble in sharing grace, mercy, and forgiveness in that it comes from you supremely, and that I remember that it is for the purpose of truth, and spirit seeds for the sake of eternal life in Christ in Jesus Name, and may all who will get on the path and in the faith of learning these things in Christ. Amen.

Additional points:

Give me humility to remember I am Human in so many different levels of mindsets and situations I face, in seeing others as human when it comes to mistakes, forgiving, redeeming, competing, in prejudice debates, when crossing paths with prejudiced enemies against one human race, when thinking that I should be able to do it all, and I need to stay in my individual human role instead of walking away from it to try and prove that I am supposedly super human or something... Help me to redeem the time Lord, and not to let pride get into my way, and show me how to redeem the time, and to be in my role, and I know that humility is one way to make sure I do not get out of my role in the body of Christ for this generation for both the saved and the lost who need to feel your tough through people of faith in Christ, and through the words of truth reaching them truth being spoken and written for your offered gift of eternal comfort...

36) Say / Pray = I accept everything from God in Christ that He gives me, already offers me, and will give me through my requests.

37) FITTING PRIVATE PRAYER: God, help us to realize how we are different, not because of our haters, but from knowing what our spiritual gift is, and what our duty is. Many of us have a spiritual path that reaches different People in various parts of society, in various cultures, with various obstacles, and sometimes in various sabotaged traps. Help us not to hate on other Christians who may have a spiritual gift that put them on the front line of helping the sabotaged, help those who are on the front line of helping the sabotaged to have more clarity, and to be more sure footed, rather than always being paranoid and busy about having to defend why they have a compassion for the sabotaged; help People to be able to recognize their duties with more clarity, and to be able to make their case to themselves, and mostly for the sake of those in bondage, and help haters of People to awaken to discontinuing the creation of bondage for others, and for People with the spiritual gifts to deal with those People and the gifts to help defend those who are called to the front lines of helping the sabotaged. Help people who deal with sabotage not to psychologically, or physically fall into the same traps that they are hoping to release, and pray that other Christians help to make path's into the Army camps easier to get in and out of rather than creating a more unpleasant and riskier mission. And pray protection of the full armor of God, and for God to oppress enemies while in a battle for the freedom to speak and share Christ's peace-loving redemption and neighborly commands. Amen.

Chapter 5 = Promote 'Spirit & Truth' Awakening Revivals

A) God Is Love - Jesus Proved It.
B) One Human Race In God's Image - Evolution Is A Lie.
C) Abortion Is Murder
D) Christ's Heaven Over Hell Is A Choice
E) Corrupt Government Power Opposes Natural Parenthood Laws
F) "Ten Commandments" > Flawed + Corrupt Medicinal Laws
G) "Golden Rule" Justice Reconciliation System

A) God Is Love - Jesus Proved It:

"'GOD IS LOVE' - JESUS PROVED IT - TRUTH AWAKENING"

Jesus said in Matthew 5:17,18, 20, 21, 22-24 "Think not that I am come to destroy the law, or the prophets: I am come not to destroy, but to fulfill. 18 For verily I say unto you, 'Till heaven and earth pass, one jot or one tittle shall in no wise pass from the law, till all be fulfilled, 20 For I say unto you, That except your righteousness shall exceed the righteousness of the scribes and Pharisees, ye shall in no case enter into the kingdom of heaven. 21 Ye have heard that it was said of them of old time, Thou shalt not kill; and whosoever shall kill shall be in danger of the judgment: 22 But I say unto you, That whosoever is angry with his brother without a cause shall be in danger of the judgment: and whosoever shall say to his brother, Raca, shall be in danger of the council: but whosoever shall say, Thou fool, shall be in danger of hell fire. 23 Therefore if thou bring thy gift to the altar, and there remember that thy brother hath ought against thee; 24 Leave there thy gift before the altar, and go thy way; first be reconciled to thy brother, and then come and offer thy gift."

John 4:23-24 "But the hour cometh, and is now, when the true worshippers shall worship the Father in spirit and in truth: for the Father seeks such to worship him. 24 God is a spirit: and they that worship him must worship him in spirit and in truth."

1 John 4:8 "He that loves not, knows not God, for God is love."

John 3:17 "For God sent not His Son into the World to condemn the World but that the World through Him might be saved."

John 3:16 "For God so loved the World that He gave His only begotten Son, that whosoever believeth in Him should not perish, but have everlasting life."

Romans 10:9,10 "That if thou shalt confess with thy mouth the Lord Jesus, and believe that God hath raised Him from the dead, thou shalt be saved."

1 John 1:8-10 If we say that we have no sin, we deceive ourselves, and the truth is not in us. 9 If we confess our sins, he is faithful and just to forgive us our sins, and to cleanse us from all unrighteousness. 10 If we say that we have not sinned, we make him a liar, and his word is not in us.

John 8 - Rebuke Pharisee-ism like Jesus did in John chapter 8.

Directives for the "'God Is Love' - Jesus Proved It Truth Awakening":

1) All churches who believe in Jesus Christ as one with God the Father who raised Him from the dead should be supportive of one another; and Jesus founded the Church, so churches who do not follow after Jesus, should be pressured by true believing Churches.

2) Church names for new churches should indicate something about God or the Truth of the Bible, or Jesus redemptive power, resurrection, or Grace: Example: Grace Bible Church, Jesus Eternal Life Church, Jesus Godhead Church, Spirit And Truth Bible Church, Peter's Bible Church, Christ's Church, Christ's Redeemed Church, Christ's Salvation Church, Jesus' Everlasting Word Church, Everlasting Bible Church, Jesus' Sanctified Church, Jesus Word Church, Jesus Life Church, Jesus Way Church, Jesus Truth Church, Jesus Faith Church, Jesus Rock Church, Christ's Rock Of Faith Church, Jesus Restoration Church, God's Grace Church, Christ's Lordship Church...New York Christian Church, Bible Christian Church, Grace Christian Church, Georgia Christian Church

(Keep in mind Pharisee-ism will continue to be brought to light more...therefore the word Christian can return to its rightful definition)

GET THE IDEA? These names are more descriptive of Jesus Church than Baptist, Presbyterian, Methodist, Episcopalian, Lutheran, and other names...

3) Every Christ believing Church should have a Bible pantry for people, and members to give Bibles to, and should have a Bible giving ministry.

Bible giving is not just something for Gideonites; it is rightfully a local Church ministry, and if people are questioning their churches sincerity or accuracy on some things...THEN THEY CAN ALWAYS BE CONFIDENT that they are giving directly to the WORD OF GOD by helping the "Bible Giving Ministry".

ALSO...local churches in every city, and county can do some work together in this effort, AND YES, it should grow to make Bibles available Worldwide from overflow in these programs... Overflow is not a problem. There is another Generation after ours, and usually the Bibles will be beginners Bibles, low budget Bibles, and once people have a low budget Bible, they will be interested in buying their own special study Bibles.

4) Point four supports point three. Every church should have a 'Food Pantry' that offers food, and also offers food to the local city food banks. WHAT TYPE OF FOOD? The foods should NOT be donuts or other unhealthy foods, BUT RATHER, the food should be Lentils, Kidney Beans, White Rice, and other efficient, non-perishable foods which can endure transport well in case of overflow.

Churches can tell city Food Banks that they will not give them food unless they put up a Bible stand in their Food Banks, and place their free Bibles on their stands... otherwise, people can come to the Churches for food, and get their Bibles there. AND YES, the Church food pantry should make food storage overflow available toward helping people overseas also, and will connect local Churches in communities through these basic programs, of sharing the Bible, and food for the needy.

5) Christians, and Churches need to remember to teach, and speak about God's person, and character, because God is who we are promoting, and He is the creator of everything purely attractive in this World. The power of attraction is in God's character and is are holy and peaceful attractions. God's love is the core of His character... and He rewards us with peace of the soul.

Some verses that support God's character and personality are: 2 Timothy 2:17 (love, joy, sound mind); 1 John 4:8 (God is love); Ephesians 4:30-32 (holy, kind, tenderhearted, forgiving) John 3:16,17 (loved the world, and came to restore not to condemn); Romans 10:9,10 (Salvation); 1 John 1:9 (God forgives sin if we confess); Genesis 18 and 19 (God showed patience and mercy with Sodom, but in the end, He showed His power and Sovereignty over the unrepentant city of Sodom).

What is most important is to speak on God's character not ours...and it is usually other people who trap us into talking about our character either to give us a failing, or passing grade, and God is the one who people need to know; there is never a failing grade in promoting the love and sovereignty of God by the repentant believer in Christ.

6) Christians should love and accept the repentance of one another, and the lost; Christian's should not reject repentance; not even for a repeated offense. People crawl before they walk; and their crawls should not be extended by other Christians rejecting repentance, and pushing them back down...God saves people in part toward the ability to exemplify His voice of forgiveness, love, redemption, and salvation. God's Word is the light we

reflect when we SPEAK His Word...that is the most direct reflection of His light, and when we speak the Word - we the follow the Word... we are reflecting the action of the Word = Forgiveness, mercy, grace, love, working to show these things. IT IS NOT how fast and articulate we are that is a reflection of God, certainly we should pursue things decently, and orderly, but that starts with the 'Rock' foundation faith in Christ's power over death as God.

7) Rest in eternal peace, and knowing that God is the only God, and Creator of all mankind. We should not fall for racial divisions. God created one Human race as corroborated by the Worldwide flood of Noah's time. We can rest in knowing that the only division that God brings is between Heaven, and Hell, and God and Satan, and Believers, and non-believers pursuit of righteousness from pursuit of sin, which may be exemplified in dividing Pharisees from Christians, and Hypocrites from Christians, and Atheists from Christians even within immediate family; and yet Christians have eternal peace, and peace of knowledge and wisdom in knowing who we are as one Creation of God who has a choice between God's love and wisdom, or Satan's hate, and confusion.

8) God is the Creator of Government. Christ is in everything. Good governance does not happen without "Loving your neighbor as yourself"; Good Governance does not happen without reverencing, and fearing God; God is where wisdom is found. In America we are "One Nation Under God" and specifically under Creation's God as written in "The Declaration Of Independence". Creation's God is both the Father of Adam and the Father of Jesus, and He is the Father of all good things, and Creator of Heaven and Earth. We have freedom of Religion, and Freedom of Speech in America; and if we did not, that would be forcing ignorance upon the people.

So, Speak, and (Mark 16:15) "...Go ye into all the world, and preach the gospel to every creature." (Matthew 28:19-20) "Go ye therefore, and teach all nations, baptizing them in the name of the Father, and of the Son, and of the Holy Ghost: 20 Teaching them to observe all things whatsoever I have commanded you: and, lo, I am with you always, even unto the end of the world. Amen."

John 8: Jesus rebuke's Pharisee-ism:

Matthew 5:17-20 (17)"Think not that I am come to destroy the law, or the prophets: I am not come to destroy, but to fulfill." (20) For I say unto you, That except your righteousness shall exceed the righteousness of the scribes and Pharisees, ye shall in no case enter into the kingdom of Heaven."

"Reality Harmonizer Bob"

B) One Human Race In God's Image - Evolution Is A Lie!

Stop hallucinating evolution = No Human has ever evolved; we all face physical death.

God created all Humans in His image through Adam and Eve, and the worldwide flood of Noah's time completely disproves evolution while also validating that we all could have come from Adam and Eve just like we all came from Noah's family after the flood.

Our various Ethnicities come from the same Human race from Noah's family who were dispersed by God at the time of "The Tower Of Babel" in Babylonia. God gave various languages at that time, and before that there was only one language. Ethnicity came about by ancestors of Noah's family moving to various regions of the World in groups according to language.

"Reality Harmonizer Bob"

C) Abortion Is Murder!

There is no honest way of getting around it - A Human baby is in the womb of a Human woman NOT a Teddy Bear or anything else, and killing that innocent Baby in the womb after conception is the murder of a Human Baby.

Conception is sacred as shown by God supernaturally putting the seed of David into Mary's womb the virgin Mother of Jesus Christ. Once the male seed enters the egg of a woman successfully, a Human life is formed and is growing.

Conception is sacred, and being pro-life in every facet of life is the direction that people are supposed to reconcile, and is the proper way of any authority to govern.

"Reality Harmonizer Bob"

D) Christ's Heaven Over Hell Is A Choice:

This is a very simple concept = If we choose to reject the resurrection power in Christ as Lord of all, then we have rejected eternal Heaven and have accepted an eternal Hell in separation from God and His Heaven which is for all who believe in resurrected Christ as Lord of all eternity.

"Reality Harmonizer Bob"

E) Corrupt Government Power Opposes Natural Parenthood Laws:

Government is scheming when government officials oppose natural parenthood laws. Think about it - Government officials who oppose God and natural family success like their own authority, and are prone to desire too much power over the citizen.

Godless Government does NOT care about gay people or any people - Government uses this issue to promote a Communist State by attempting to redefine what a parent is. If Government were completely successful at redefining parenthood and marriage, then Government would have the power to take any children it wants, and to place them anywhere it wants, because there would be no such thing as a real natural parent, but rather a child only would belong where the Government would say so.

Do not fall for a greedy Politicians trick that favors stranger guardians over natural parents...

"Reality Harmonizer Bob"

F) "Ten Commandments" > Flawed, Corrupt Medicinal Laws

For many years now the USA and much of the world has highly valued flawed medicinal laws often CREATED by the false Scientists who claim evolution, and police have prioritized those corrupt laws while ignoring God's "Ten Commandments" of 'thou shalt not steal'...

Well, the police need to start holding the mafia's, street gangs, Scientists, and everyone else far more accountable to God's "Ten Commandments" protecting private property of people and protect against violent threats whether people are sober or not, and insist on true Science coming up with safer forms of street medicines + creating better anti-addiction medicines...

God's "Ten Commandments" from Moses tell us what to prioritize in Loving God and Loving our neighbors... and the Bible does NOT say 'thou shalt not steal except from someone who uses a medicine'. Stealing is never okay.

I believe that false racist evolution "Scientists" run most of the medicinal science field, and they have scared real Scientists away from experimenting with medicines, and they have intentionally NOT done the job of creating good low dose / low potency medicines which they can influence legalization of, and help to get people off of illegal street drugs, and to help put illegal drug dealers out of business who deal swindler forms, and often laced drug forms that are not intended to help people but rather are intended to trick the psyche. Let real God-fearing, one Human race believing Scientists explore the medicine world and create better venues and influence better laws, and get rid of the huge trickery sobriety obstruction lie of "once an addict always an addict"; physical addiction phase of anything can usually be broken in 3 days, and if people stick it out through the 3 days of pain and fatigue withdrawals, they typically don't want to have to go through that again, but most don't realize it only takes 3 days, because of the "once and addict, always an addict" deception.

"Reality Harmonizer Bob"

G) "Golden Rule" Justice Reconciliation System:

Prison reform and Judicial systems need major improvements and repair. These are not areas that people think about much today for a variety of reasons - one being that many people tend to stereotype others as criminals and simply think they get what they deserve, or that locking them up and throwing away the key keeps the public safe, BUT it is a lot more complex than that.

Locking people up and throwing away the key, over punishing, and other things like that creates more problems than it solves.

The Bible commands "The Golden Rule" of "Do to others as you would have them do unto you" if you were the one caught in a fault... (Matthew 7:12; Luke 6:31)

"Over punishing is stealing." That is a quote from me - "Reality Harmonizer Bob", but is a revelation that is similar to the old American standard of "may the punishment fit the crime".

PROPER JUSTICE is under God in that we recognize all people are Human with Human imperfection, and recognizes that Human's need guidance, and Human's need to recognize God their Creator, AND that in justice assessment we first need to FORGIVE, THEN discern what is a proper punishment, correction and/or redemptive reconciliation process for both the suspect and the victim... (not all cases are the same...)

Another area that needs improvement in the justice system is the lengthy court system. It should rarely ever take more than a few weeks to 6 months to finish a case - long drawn-out court cases are often about money for Lawyers, Judges, and the Prosecution side, and no one should ever be rewarded more than 7 times the value of anything.

Another area that needs improvement is the prison process = PRISON'S SHOULD IN FACT BE HUMANE = A prison is supposed to be a place of reconciliation in a nation "under God". So, showers should be more private, people should be expected to use diplomacy rather than to fight and bully, people should be expected to be treated well by Police and to treat Police well... people should be preparing for a sane release, learning and gaining a taste for peacemaking skills, and embarking upon substantial employment once released; and should get early release for good behavior after finding employment rather than release being based on a money system (except on minor infractions) which often releases people for money with no rehabilitation, and can become a irrationally rationalized money making scheme.

Being detained is already plenty of punishment - Prison's should be a Humane reconciliation process, and should not create years of debt for people on probation - The reconciliation system should be a Non-Profit organization as should the Justice system and Policing departments.

Chapter 6 = Misconception Nonconformist Principles

1) Forgive first, then discern an issue whether individual or an authority like courts...

2) Matthew 6:33-34 "But seek ye first the kingdom of God, and His righteousness; and all these things shall be added unto you. 34) Take therefore no thought for the morrow: for the morrow shall take thought for the things of itself. Sufficient unto the day is the evil thereof."

3) James 4:14-15 "Whereas you do not know what will happen tomorrow. For what is your life? It is even a vapor that appears for a little time and then vanishes away. 15 Instead you ought to say, "If the Lord wills, we shall live and do this or that."

4) 1 Peter 3:10 "Whoever desires to love life and see good days, let him keep his tongue from evil and his lips from speaking deceit."

5) Romans 12:1-2 "I beseech you therefore, brethren, by the mercies of God, that ye present your bodies a living sacrifice, holy, acceptable unto God, which is your reasonable service. 2) And be not conformed to this world but be ye transformed by the renewing of your mind, that ye may prove what is that good, and acceptable, and perfect, will of God."

6) Romans 12:14 "Bless them which persecute you: bless, and curse not."

Matthew 5:44 "But I say unto you, Love your enemies, bless them that curse you, do good to them that hate you, and pray for them which despitefully use you, and persecute you;"

7) Romans 12:17 "Recompense to no man evil for evil. Provide things honest in the sight of all."

8) Romans 12:18 "If it be possible, as much as is in you, live peaceably with all men."

9) Psalm 1:1-2 "Blessed is the man that walks not in the counsel of the ungodly, nor stands in the way of sinners, nor sits in the seat of the scornful. 2) But his delight is in the law of the Lord; and in His law doth he meditate day and night."

10) Proverbs 1:7 "The fear of the Lord is the beginning of knowledge: but fools despise wisdom and instruction."

11) Proverbs 1:10 "My son, if sinners entice thee, consent thou not."

12) Proverbs 3:5-6 "Trust in the Lord with all thine heart, and lean not unto thine own understanding. 6) In all thy ways acknowledge Him, and He shall

direct thy paths."

13) 2 Timothy 2:15 "Study to shew thyself approved unto God, a workman that needs not to be ashamed, rightly dividing the word of truth."

14) Mark 8:36 "For what shall it profit a man, if he shall gain the whole world, and lose his own soul?"

15) Mark 8:38 Christ speaking, "Whosoever therefore shall be ashamed of me and of my words in this adulterous and sinful generation; of him also shall the Son of man be ashamed when He cometh in the glory of His Father with the holy angels."

16) Luke 14:26-27 Jesus speaking, "If any man come to me, and hate not his father, and mother, and wife, and children, and brethren, and sisters, yea, and his own life also, he cannot be my disciple. 27) And whosoever doth not bear his cross, and come after me, cannot be my disciple." (hate is based on comparison to loving Christ, based on hating vain things others want for you if it is contrary to what Christ wants...)

17) Matthew 5:3 "Blessed are the poor in spirit: for theirs is the kingdom of heaven."

18) Matthew 5:5 "Blessed are the meek: for they shall inherit the earth."

19) Matthew 5:9 "Blessed are the peacemakers: for they shall be called the children of God."

20) Matthew 5:17-18 "Think not that I am come to destroy the law, or the prophets: I am not come to destroy, but to fulfill." 18)"For verily I say unto you, 'Till heaven and earth pass, one jot or one tittle shall in no wise pass from the law, till all be fulfilled."

21) Matthew 5:21-24 "Ye have heard that it was said of them of old time, Thou shalt not kill; and whosoever shall kill shall be in danger of the judgment 22) "But I say unto you, That whosoever is angry with his brother without a cause shall be in danger of the judgment: and whosoever shall say to his brother, Raca, shall be in danger of the council: but whosoever shall say, Thou fool, shall be in danger of hell fire." 23) Therefore if thou bring thy gift to the altar, and there remembers that thy brother hath ought against thee; 24) Leave there thy gift before the altar, and go thy way; first be reconciled to thy brother, and then come and offer thy gift."

22) Matthew 22:36-40 "Master, which is the greatest commandment in the law? 37) Jesus said unto him, Thou shalt love the Lord thy God with all thy heart, and with all thy soul, and with all thy mind. 38) This is the first and great commandment. 39) And the second is like unto it, Thou shalt love thy neighbor as thyself. 40) On these two commandments hang all the law and the prophets."

23) God's "Ten Commandments" are profitable in many ways. Not only should we adhere and teach ourselves and our children and neighbors and enemies not to steal, but we should also read that commandment as "thou shalt not steal my stuff either"... The commandments are there to protect other's lives, and our own, and will be enforced 100% to protect the eternal heavens.

24) Galatians 5:16 "This I say then, walk in the Spirit, and ye shall not fulfill the lust of the flesh."

25) Ecclesiastes 12:1 "Remember now thy Creator in the days of thy youth, while the evil days come not, nor the years draw nigh, when thou shalt say, I have no pleasure in them:"

26) Ecclesiastes 12:11-14 "The words of the wise are as goads, and as nails fastened by the masters of assemblies, which are given from one shepherd. 12) And further, by these, my son, be admonished: of making many books there is no end; and much study is a weariness of the flesh. 13) Let us hear the conclusion of the whole matter: Fear God, and keep his commandments: for this is the whole duty of man. 14) For God shall bring every work into judgment, with every secret thing, whether it be good, or whether it be evil."

27) Matthew 7:15 "Beware of false prophets, which come to you in sheep's clothing, but inwardly they are ravening wolves."

28) Ezekiel 13:3 "Thus says the Lord God; Woe unto the foolish prophets, that follow their own spirit, and have seen nothing!"

29) James 1:27 "Pure religion and undefiled before God and the Father is this, to visit the fatherless and widows in their affliction, and to keep himself unspotted from the world."

30) James 1:8 "A double minded man is unstable in all his ways."

31) James 1:13-15 "Let no man say when he is tempted, I am tempted of

God: for God cannot be tempted with evil, neither tempts he any man: 14) But every man is tempted, when he is drawn away of his own lust, and enticed. 15) Then when lust hath conceived, it brings forth sin: and sin, when it is finished, brings forth death."

32) James 2:1 "My brethren, have not the faith of our Lord Jesus Christ, the Lord of glory, with respect of persons."

33) James 2:26 "For as the body without the spirit is dead, so faith without works is dead also."

34) James 3:13-18 "Who is a wise man and endued with knowledge among you? let him shed out of a good conversation his works with meekness of wisdom. 14) But if ye have bitter envying and strife in your hearts, glory not, and lie not against the truth. 15) This wisdom descends not from above, but is earthly, sensual, devilish. 16) For where envying and strife is, there is confusion and every evil work. 17) But the wisdom that is from above is first pure, then peaceable, gentle, and easy to be intreated, full of mercy and good fruits, without partiality, and without hypocrisy. 18) And the fruit of righteousness is sown in peace of them that make peace."

35) James 4:7-10 "Submit yourselves therefore to God. Resist the devil, and he will flee from you. 8) Draw nigh to God, and He will draw night to you. Cleanse your hands, ye sinners; and purify your hearts, ye double minded. 9) Be afflicted, and mourn, and weep: let your laughter be turned to mourning, and your joy to heaviness. 10) Humble yourselves in the sight of the Lord, and He shall lift you up."

36) James 4:17 "Therefore to him that knows to do good, and doeth it not, to him it is sin."

37) James 5:19-20 "Brethren, if any of you do err from the truth, and one convert him; 20) Let him know, that he which converts the sinner from the error of his way shall save a soul from death, and shall hide a multitude of sins."

38) Hebrews 12:1-2 "Wherefore seeing we also are compassed about with so great a cloud of witnesses, let us lay aside every weight, and the sin which doth so easily beset us, and let us run with patience the race that is set before us, 2) Looking unto Jesus the author and finisher of our faith; who for the joy that was set before him endured the cross, despising the shame, and is set down at the right hand of the throne of God."

39) 1 Corinthians 6:2-3 "Do ye not know that the saints shall judge the world? And if the world shall be judged by you, are ye unworthy to judge the smallest matters? 3) Know ye not that we shall judge angels? How much more things that pertain to this life?"

40) 1 Corinthians 13 whole chapter, but will site the first and last verse here = 1) "Though I speak with the tongues of men and of angels, and have not love, I am like a sounding brass or cymbal playing no song (paraphrase rewording) 13) And now abides faith, hope, love, these three; but the greatest of these is love (charity)."

CHAPTER 7 = 'SPIRIT & TRUTH' AWARENESS CALENDAR

JOHN 4:24 - "God is a Spirit: and they that worship Him must worship Him in Spirit and in truth."

JANUARY = "'Spirit & Truth' Evaluation Month"
FEBRUARY = "'Lincoln's Victory Celebration Month"

MARCH = "Sacred Conception Celebration Month"
APRIL = "Pro-Life Celebration Month"

MAY = "Natural Parental Responsibility Month"
JUNE = "Natural Adoption Awareness Month"
JULY = "Neighborly Justice Awareness Month"

AUGUST = "Evangelistic History Month" (Peter, Paul, John Wesley, Martin Luther, Billy Sunday, Billy Graham, D.L. Moody, George Washington Carver, Charles Hadden Spurgeon, Martin Luther King Jr, Bible reading freedom celebration...)

SEPTEMBER = "Ethnicity History Month"
OCTOBER = "Holy Ghost Celebration Month"
NOVEMBER = "Creations Gratefulness Month"
DECEMBER = "One Human Race Celebration Month"

Chapter 8 = Change For Christ's Kingdom

    Some things Christ says seem to be different than the way an avid examiner would interpret "The Ten Commandments", BUT I do NOT think Jesus interpretation to be a contradiction, nor very difficult to understand, because His admonishment is from a perspective of mercy and forgiveness toward the hope of advancing His redeeming love for the sake of Heaven's new birth's.

    Am I correct? Well, in part at least, because some of what Christ shared certainly goes over my head, but makes sense in the way of mercy and compassion. Howbeit, I think I am certainly correct to protect "Thou shalt not Kill, steal, covet, or bear false witness against neighbors", and to seek ways of discernment in promoting just enforcement of those commandments on this earth.

    Christ states in "The Lord's Prayer" that we should pray "Thy Kingdom Come, Thy will be done on earth as it is in Heaven." (Matthew 6:10) So, from that reference and other references in the Bible I derive that God wants us to help present and give a presence of His Heavenly Kingdom on Earth, and to me that means in part that we need to protect "The Ten Commandments" on earth for peaceable living, and because in Heaven those commandments will be enforced 100%.

    Christ simplifies the law for us, and helps us to know better how to interpret it in Matthew 22:35-40:

35 Then one of them, which was a lawyer, asked him a question, tempting him, and saying,
36 Master, which is the great commandment in the law?
37 Jesus said unto him, Thou shalt love the Lord thy God with all thy heart, and with all thy soul, and with all thy mind.
38 This is the first and great commandment.
39 And the second is like unto it, Thou shalt love thy neighbour as thyself.
40 On these two commandments hang all the law and the prophets.

Below is a portion of my observational perspective in valuing "The Ten Commandments":

1) There are no politics better than Christ's 'Ten Commandments', and Christ tells us in Matthew 22, that "all other commandments hang on these two, Love God with all your heart, soul, and mind, and love your neighbor as yourself".

2) Christ's commandment of "Thou shalt not steal" is more valuable than money and other property, without that command no one has any money or property of their own.

3) Christ's commandment of "Thou shalt not murder" gives value to life, and without that command, there would be little, if any sustained life. Christ talks in Matthew 22 about "being angry without a cause as being as guilty as the sin of murder, and calls for immediate repentance from that anger".

4) "The Ten Commandments" are a grace gift from God for the protection of every single human being, and for a glimpse of what Heaven will be like where the commandments will be perfectly enforced.

5) Personalize "The Ten Commandments" = They were NOT just written for us to check our own behavior by, nor simply to govern by, but also to personalize in this way = "Thou shalt not kill me, Thou shalt not covet my stuff, Thou shalt not steal from me, Thou shalt not lie about me"... You are supposed to love me, your human neighbor...

6) God's Neighbor Laws (Ten Commandments) > Flawed Science laws which do not value our neighbors.

7) If you cannot love your enemy then you cannot love yourself, because we are all our most frequent enemy, and we are doing pretty good if we are not our own worst enemy which rejects God in Christ.

8) Do not forget that "Loving God wholly" is the top commandment. If we are not remembering and revering "under God" in any thought, any thought or way is sure to get twisted without acknowledging God's Holy Spirit. Galatians 5:22-23 "But the fruit of the Spirit is love, joy, peace, longsuffering (patience), gentleness, goodness, faith, meekness, temperance: against such there is no law."

Bottom line, Christ not only tells us to keep "The Ten Commandments" but He also eludes for us to repent of the thoughts, spirits, and attitudes that lead to breaking "The Ten Commandments", and He tells us to forgive and reconcile with both God and man, friend, or enemy, guilty or innocent.

Howbeit, God gave us "The Ten Commandments" as the law foundation for governing a nation, governing family, and governing ourselves, and Christ further taught us how to apply "The Ten Commandments" mentally, and with forgiveness, mercy and redemptive, reconciliatory justice.

I will end this chapter by giving 2 Scripture passages. One passage is Exodus 20 where you will read "The Ten Commandments", and the other passage is Psalm 1 telling us that it is blessed to meditate in the law of the Lord day and night, and the one comment I want to make about Psalm 1 is to recognize that we do not need to focus on our enemies, but we need to focus on the Law of the Lord.

Exodus 20:1-20

1 And God spake all these words, saying,
2 I am the Lord thy God, which have brought thee out of the land of Egypt, out of the house of bondage.
3 Thou shalt have no other gods before me.
4 Thou shalt not make unto thee any graven image, or any likeness of any thing that is in heaven above, or that is in the earth beneath, or that is in the water under the earth.
5 Thou shalt not bow down thyself to them, nor serve them: for I the Lord thy God am a jealous God, visiting the iniquity of the fathers upon the children unto the third and fourth generation of them that hate me;
6 And shewing mercy unto thousands of them that love me, and keep my commandments.
7 Thou shalt not take the name of the Lord thy God in vain; for the Lord will not hold him guiltless that taketh his name in vain.
8 Remember the sabbath day, to keep it holy.
9 Six days shalt thou labour, and do all thy work:
10 But the seventh day is the sabbath of the Lord thy God: in it thou shalt not do any work, thou, nor thy son, nor thy daughter, thy manservant, nor thy maidservant, nor thy cattle, nor thy stranger that is within thy gates:
11 For in six days the Lord made heaven and earth, the sea, and all that in them is, and rested the seventh day: wherefore the Lord blessed the sabbath day, and hallowed it.
12 Honour thy father and thy mother: that thy days may be long upon the land which the Lord thy God giveth thee.
13 Thou shalt not kill.
14 Thou shalt not commit adultery.

15 Thou shalt not steal.
16 Thou shalt not bear false witness against thy neighbour.
17 Thou shalt not covet thy neighbour's house, thou shalt not covet thy neighbour's wife, nor his manservant, nor his maidservant, nor his ox, nor his ass, nor any thing that is thy neighbour's.
18 And all the people saw the thunderings, and the lightnings, and the noise of the trumpet, and the mountain smoking: and when the people saw it, they removed, and stood afar off.
19 And they said unto Moses, Speak thou with us, and we will hear: but let not God speak with us, lest we die.
20 And Moses said unto the people, Fear not: for God is come to prove you, and that his fear may be before your faces, that ye sin not.

Psalm 1

1 Blessed is the man that walketh not in the counsel of the ungodly, nor standeth in the way of sinners, nor sitteth in the seat of the scornful.
2 But his delight is in the law of the Lord; and in his law doth he meditate day and night.
3 And he shall be like a tree planted by the rivers of water, that bringeth forth his fruit in his season; his leaf also shall not wither; and whatsoever he doeth shall prosper.
4 The ungodly are not so: but are like the chaff which the wind driveth away.
5 Therefore the ungodly shall not stand in the judgment, nor sinners in the congregation of the righteous.
6 For the Lord knoweth the way of the righteous: but the way of the ungodly shall perish.

"Be as selfish as 'The Ten Commandments' allow you to be = 'thou shalt not covet MY STUFF', but also be gracious and merciful like Christ compels you to be." "Reality Harmonizer" Bob

"Christ's politics matter most."

CHAPTER 9 = Quotes for Clothing, Accessories & Whatever (1-1114)

1) Trust + teach Christ saves.

2) Rise with Christ.

3) Invest in Heaven.

4) Love repentance.

5) God's image not evolution.

6) One Human race from Noah's Ark.

7) God's image.

8) Created in God's image.

9) Evolution is a racist lie.

10) Trust G-C-S = God-Christ's-Spirit.

11) Warn about Hell.

12) Do not choose Hell.

13) Urgent warning: Choose Heaven not Hell.

14) Celebrate Lincoln ending slavery.

15) "Under God" = under Mercy.

16) "Under God" = under Discernment.

17) "Under God" = under Humility.

18) Truth matters.

19) Natural Fatherhood matters.

20) God-Christ's-Spirit matters.

21) Babies matter.

22) Racial unity matters.

23) "Under God" = racial Unity

24) One Human race is only acknowledged "under God".

25) Loving God matters most.

26) Own property via God's ten.

27) Pursue truth.

28) Pursue truth = pursue reality.

29) Enter Heaven = Presently enter Christ's forgiveness and salvation.

30) Various Ethnicity's, but only one Human race under God.

31) No forgiveness = no life.

32) Be repetitious in forgiveness.

33) Be repetitious sharing life's truth.

34) Be repetitious seeking wisdom.

35) Be repetitious sharing Christ.

36) Be repetitious in teaching the Gospel.

37) Be repetitious in Heaven's sake.

38) Encourage redemption.

39) Encourage restoration.

40) Encourage reconciliation.

41) Encourage forgiveness.

42) Encourage eternal salvation.

43) Encourage repentance.

44) Encourage neighborliness.

45) Encourage peacemaking.

46) Encourage diplomacy.

47) Encourage neighborly justice.

48) Encourage moral freedom.

49) Encourage private prayer.

50) Encourage genuine prayer.

51) Encourage natural Fatherhood.

52) Encourage natural Parenthood.

53) Encourage natural marriage.

53) Encourage natural Parent responsibility.

54) Encourage natural family adoption.

55) Encourage private property rights.

56) Encourage redemptive justice.

57) Encourage discernment.

58) Encourage wisdom.

59) Encourage truth.

60) Encourage Christ's "Golden Rule."

61) Encourage eternal compassion.

62) Encourage sober mindedness.

63) Encourage vigilance.

64) Encourage Godly loving pursuits.

65) Encourage pursuit of righteousness.

66) Encourage patience.

67) Encourage temperance.

68) Encourage Spirit + Truth worship.

69) Encourage eternal faith.

70) Encourage resurrection faith.

71) Encourage eternal joy.

72) Encourage Christ's hope.

73) Encourage mercy.

74) Encourage eternal hope.

75) Encourage meekness.

76) Encourage revering God.

77) Encourage truth pursuit.

78) Encourage loving God.

79) Encourage Gods laws.

80) Encourage understanding "Under God".

81) Encourage Godly focus.

82) Encourage charity.

83) Encourage stewardship.

84) Encourage appetite temperance.

86) Encourage being Spirit-filled.

87) Stop hallucinating Evolution.

88) Encourage property protection.

89) God wants everyone.

90) Conception is sacred.

92) Umbilical cord is a sovereign evidenced lifeline.

93) Encourage Biblical meditation.

94) Choose Heaven not Hell.

96) Choose Heavens power, not your own.

97) Choose repentance.

98) Choose Humility "under God".

99) Choose Christ's Heaven.

100) Trust revelation faith.

102) Trust Gods Baby revelation.

103) Trust Gods cross forgiveness revelation.

104) Trust Gods ascension power revelation.

105) Choose Gods ascension power revelation.

106) Choose Gods cross forgiveness revelation.

107) Choose Gods cross forgiveness.

108) Trust eternal pro-life. tTt

109) Choose eternal pro-life. tTt

110) Forbid Baby slaughterhouses.

111) Love your mate not abortion.

112) Property rights are more valuable than money.

113) Christ proved God is Love.

114) Christ showed that He is God.

115) "Under God" = under true wisdom.

116) Loves label = Jesus Christ.

117) Proper population control = Nations honoring Gods "10 Commandments".

118) Evolution is racist.

119) Evolution is racism.

120) Defund Evolution.

121) Outlaw the racist Evolution theory lie.

122) Abolish Evolution.

123) Outlaw Evolution.

124) Ban Evolution in School.

125) Teach Creation not Evolution.

126) Teach one Human race not Evolution.

127) God created Human equality.

128) God created one Human race.

129) God created Human anatomy.

130) God created gender.

131) God created you.

132) Plan natural parenthood.

133) True planned parenthood loves babies.

134) Plan Fatherhood + Motherhood.

135) Independence Globalist under G-C-S.

136) Independence Globalist "under God."

137) Independence Globalist "under God-Christ's-Spirit."

138) Natural Parenthood matters.

139) Real Doctors save lives.

140) Babies are Human.

141) Abortion is murder.

142) Abolish abortion.

143) Outlaw abortion.

144) Outlaw Baby slaughterhouses.

145) Outlaw Abortionists.

146) Outlaw Abortion clinics.

147) A womb is not a tomb.

148) A Womb = a child's first room.

149) Democrats are racist.

150) Only Democrats owe reparations.

151) Christ is God - Colossians 1.

152) Trust God-Christ's-Spirit.

153) Police yourself - don't hate Police.

154) Celebrate Lincoln's victory.

155) Sealed in God's blood.

156) Reach for God over Stars.

157) Trust Heavens quality.

158) Human under God.

159) Forgiven under God.

160) Property rights matter.

161) Border security matters.

163) G-C-S Saves.

164) Satan works for evil; work for good.

165) Life is not a crime.

166) Wisdom walks with the forgiving.

167) Life would not exist without forgiveness.

168) Extreme insanity rejects Christ.

169) Hell is unforgiving; choose forgiveness.

170) Be as selfish as Gods 10 Commandments allows.

171) Love your soul not your sin.

172) Faith's source matters.

173) The best World = the next one.

174) A better World works wisely.

175) Understand God.

176) Moral freedom protects life.

177) Immoral freedom steals.

178) God is Love - Christ proved it!

179) Discriminate against Hell.

180) God's politics matter.

181) Your greatest ability is to choose Heaven.

182) Choosing Hell is insanely extreme.

183) Political conspiracy legislates Fatherless methodology.

184) Gospel music never expires.

185) Gratefulness acknowledges positivity.

186) Don't steal your peace with God.

187) Gluttony does not love us back.

188) Faith only lasts as long as its source.

189) God is the cause of faith.

190) Faith in dirt for the 2nd life is no good.

191) Faith in dead gods is no good.

192) Dead gods = dead Religions = false Religions.

193) Good Religion = Heavenly Religion = Resurrection power Religion.

194) "Freedom of Religion" NOT freedom of false Religion.

195) The best World = living forever with Christ.

196) A better World = a more neighborly World in Christ.

197) Change for Christ.

198) Change for Christ's Kingdom.

199) Think healthy; your quality-of-life matters.

200) Defy stereotyping = life is not over before 20.

201) Grade adult life properly.

202) Words matter = God created the World with words.

203) The best street fighters are dead or wounded.

204) The Human mind is vast.

205) Psychology is vast.

206) Impressions change with Seasons.

207) Worship Christ not the Bible.

208) For higher learning disagree with yourself.

209) Pray with Gospel music.

210) Believing "all have sinned" points to God as Supreme.

211) Money burns as will its lovers.

212) Money does not last, but it can count toward Heaven.

213) Be a "Non-Conformist" to Satan.

214) Be a "Non-Conformist" to misconceptions.

215) Be a "Non-Conformist" to unforgiveness.

216) Be a "Non-Conformist" to abortionists.

217) Be a "Non-Conformist" to marriage perversions.

218) Be a "Non-Conformist" to Evolution's lies.

219) Be a "Non-Conformist" to destruction.

220) Be a "Non-Conformist" to hating people.

221) Be a "Non-Conformist" to common bigotry.

222) Be a "Non-Conformist" to doubting God.

223) Be a "Non-Conformist" to staying depressed.

224) Be a "Non-Conformist" to pessimism.

225) Be a "Non-Conformist" to fantasies.

226) Be a "Non-Conformist" to delusions.

227) Be a "Non-Conformist" to lies.

228) Be a "Non-Conformist" to slander.

229) Be a "Non-Conformist" to defamation.

230) Be a "Non-Conformist" to false witness.

231) Be a "Non-Conformist" to oppression.

232) Be a "Non-Conformist" to shaming.

233) Be a "Non-Conformist" to chaos.

234) Be a "Non-Conformist" to violence.

235) Be a "Non-Conformist" to stealing.

236) Be a "Non-Conformist" to drunkenness.

237) Be a "Non-Conformist" to over punishing.

238) Be a "Non-Conformist" to revenge.

239) Be a "Non-Conformist" to injustice.

240) Be a "Non-Conformist" to bitterness.

241) Be a "Non-Conformist" to stressful thoughts.

242) Be a "Non-Conformist" to stressful thinking.

243) Be a "Non-Conformist" to unnecessary stress.

244) Be a "Non-Conformist" to unhealthy stress.

245) Be a "Non-Conformist" to Gluttony.

246) Be a "Non-Conformist" to vanity.

247) Be a "Non-Conformist" to true racism.

248) Be a "Non-Conformist" to rejecting Christ.

249) Be a "Non-Conformist" to Hell's destiny.

250) Be a "Non-Conformist" to bad Spirits.

251) Be a "Non-Conformist" to mockery.

252) Be a "Non-Conformist" to scorning.

253) Be a "Non-Conformist" to Godless religions.

254) Godless Religion is NOT Religion.

255) Be restorative with God-Christ's-Spirit.

256) Be real with God-Christ's-Spirit.

257) Be reconciling with God-Christ's-Spirit.

258) Be forgiving with God-Christ's-Spirit.

259) Be merciful with God-Christ's-Spirit.

260) Be encouraging with God-Christ's-Spirit.

261) Be hopeful with God-Christ's-Spirit.

262) Be peaceful with God -Christ's-Spirit.

263) Be good with God-Christ's-Spirit.

264) Be humble under God-Christ's-Spirit.

265) Ge graceful under God-Christ's-Spirit.

266) Be gentle under God-Christ's-Spirit.

267) Be patient under God-Christ's-Spirit.

268) Be loving with God-Christ's-Spirit.

269) Be joyful under God-Christ's-Spirit.

270) Be confident in God-Christ's-Spirit.

271) Have faith in God-Christ's-Spirit.

272) Be confident in Heavens Christ.

273) Trust in God-Christ's-Spirit.

274) Lean on Christ's truth.

275) Lean on Christ's resurrection power.

276) Lean on Christ's forgiveness.

277) Lean on Christ's salvation.

278) Lean on Christ's redemption.

279) Lean on Christ's reconciliation.

280) Follow Christ's Spirit.

281) Repent of violent thoughts in obedience to Gods Ten Commandments.

282) Repent & obey Gods Ten Commandments.

283) Repent and ask God's forgiveness.

284) Be forgiven with God-Christ's-Spirit.

285) Follow Gods fruit of the Spirit.

286) Trust Gods fruit of the Spirit.

287) Have confidence in God's fruit of the Spirit.

288) Walk in obedience to Gods Holy Spirit.

289) Walk in obedience to the fruit of the Spirit.

290) It is God's will for all to walk with the fruit of the Spirit.

291) It is God's will for all to be confident in Christ for eternal life.

292) It is God's will for all to promote & joy in Christ's salvation with all people.

293) It is God's will for all to walk in obedience to Gods Ten Commandments.

294) It is God's will for all to walk in success with Gods Ten Commandments.

295) Walk in obedience to Gods Ten Commandments.

296) Walk in success with Gods Ten Commandments.

297) Walk in success with the fruit of the Spirit.

298) Walk in success with God-Christ's-Spirit.

299) God-Christ's-Spirit saved me from Hell.

300) Christ's salvation saves from Hell for eternal life.

301) Conform to Gods commandments.

302) Conform to God-Christ's-Spirit.

303) Conform to Heavenly value.

304) Conform to eternal wealth.
305) Conform to eternal value.

306) Conform to everlasting life.

307) Conform to reconciliation.

308) Be temperate for God-Christ's-Spirit.

309) Conform to Gods loving Spirit.

310) Work for the gain not for the pain.

311) Employ to build up not to use up.

312) Work to own + work to help partners own.

313) We work as partners in the free market system.

314) Employers and Employees are systematic partners in the free market system.

315) Conform to Spirit and Truth.

316) Conform to Christ's hope.

317) Conform to Christ's forgiveness.

318) Conform to Christ's compassion.

319) Conform to Gods peace.

320) Conform to everlasting peace.

321) Conform to pure Godly love.

322) Conform to everlasting love.

323) Conform to eternal resurrection power.

324) Conform to cross forgiveness.

325) Conform to loving enemies.

326) Conform to patience with enemies.

327) Conform to not envying enemies.

328) Conform to being kind to enemies.

329) Conform to being gracious to enemies.

330) Conform to being merciful to enemies.

331) Conform to truth under God for enemies.

332) Conform to Godly hope for enemies.

333) Conform to persevering for enemies.

334) Conform to eternal faith for enemies.

335) Conform to eternal love for enemies.

336) Conform to praying for enemies.

337) Conform to forgiving enemies.

338 Conform to Godly justice for enemies.

339) Conform to fair justice for enemies.

340) Conform to merciful justice for enemies.

341) Conform to justice vs revenge for enemies.

342) Hope for salvation for enemies.

343) Hope for repentance in enemies.

344) Pray for salvation for enemies.

345) Pray for a spiritual awakening for enemies.
346) Pray for Gods peace for enemies.

347) Hope for Gods peace for enemies.

348) Pray for wisdom with enemies.

349) Pray for patience with enemies.

350) Pray for safety with enemies.

351) Pray for protection from enemies.

352) Conform to protective measures from enemies.

353) Conform to seeking wisdom.

354) Conform to being discerning.

355) Conform to sharing Christ's ways.

356) Conform to sharing Christ's salvation.

357) Conform to sharing Christ's Gospel.

358) Conform to warning People about the next life.

359) Conform to warning People about Hell.

360) Conform to sharing Heaven's choice.

361) Assume you do not know who are Friends or Foes; summarize prayer as for all Friends & Foes.

362) Holy love was seen on Christ's cross.

363) Pro-Heaven music cares.

364) Forgiveness from Christians comes from God.

365) The grass really is more enjoyable with faith in Christ.

366) Valuable faith believes in everlasting hope.

367) Give People a little bit of Heaven with fruit of Gods Spirit.

368) Give People a little bit of Heaven.

369) Give People Heavens link.

370) Christ was predestined to forgive everyone.

371) Gender destruction is not self-love.

372) Revering Gods 10 gives opportunity to experience less of Hell's destruction on Earth.

373) Dear God, change my mind.

374) Dear God, give me wisdom.

375) Dear God, give me strength.

376) Dear God, give me temperance.

377) Dear God, give me joy.

378) Dear God, give me endurance.

379) Dear God, give me patience.

380) Dear God, help my memory.

381) Dear God, intercede for me.

382) Dear God, give me intercession.

383) Dear God, help me.

384) Dear God, help my focus.

385) Dear God, enlighten blinded hearts.

386) Dear God, awaken apathetic hearts.

387) Dear God, awaken stubborn hearts.

388) Dear God, enlighten hateful hearts.

389) Dear God, enlighten unsaved souls.

390) Dear God, help me redeem time.

391) Only God is Supreme.

392) Democrat's government supremacy goals are NOT neighborly.

393) Democrat's global supremacy scheme is NOT neighborly.

394) Robots do not have free will.

395) Christ is God above all gods.

396) No God except Christ's Trinity.

397) Anyone can become more Heavenly with Christ.

398) Positive change takes diligence.

399) Positive change takes persistence.

400) Positive change takes patience.

401) Positive change takes believing Christ not Christ's doubters.

402) Positive change resists vanity.

403) Positive change confesses sin to God-Christ's-Spirit.

404) Positive change acknowledges sin to God-Christ's-Spirit.

405) Positive change repents regularly.

406) Positive change wants God's forgiveness.

407) Positive change wants God's salvation.

408) Positive change wants Christ's eternal life.

409) Positive change seeks daily communion with God-Christ's-Spirit.
410) Positive change views people as created in God's image.

411) Positive change extends God's grace to His enemies.

412) God's Human enemies are simultaneously my enemies & neighbors.

413) Genius actions connect to reality.

414) Genius actions connect to truth.

415) Anyone can be the child of Genius via trusting Heavens Genius Creator.

416) Genius actions acknowledge God persistently.

417) Genius actions acknowledge God eternally.

418) Genius actions acknowledge God as infinitely Supreme.

419) Genius actions often disagree with self.

420) Genius actions agree with God.

421) God is the Supreme Genius.

422) Don't just be a Child of the Genius; always remember God.

423) Genius starts with revering God.

424) Genius connects to God; foolishness is not tuning in.

425) Direction matters more than speed.

426) Your disgust for health food is irrelevant.

427) Stop forcing dead gods on People.

428) You cannot offend dead gods.

429) Stop offending the only Living God.

430) Opposing deception is a result of some reverence for truth.

431) The Human race does not come separately no batteries needed.

432) Democrats are not racist? And Fathers can be Mothers?

433) Please God more than People.

434) God's #1 Rule = love God; #2 Rule = love people

435) Choose good over evil and eternal pleasure over pain.

436) Unforgiveness is weird.

437) Choose golden streets.

438) Oppose conceptual lies.

439) Declare conceptual truth.

440) Share conceptual truth.

441) Declare spiritual blessings.

442) Share spiritual blessings.

443) Spiritual blessings come from trust in Christ's peace.

444) Conceptual truth comes from meditating with God in His Word.

445) Temperance reaps peace.

446) Balancing emotion for Gods Spirit and Truth brings peace.

447) Balancing appetites gives more peace.

448) God's Ten Commandments are a piece of Heaven.

449) The Free-Market System lets us choose jobs lets us change jobs.

450) Godly heart reverence cannot be seen, but is detectable.

451) Trust Heaven's only revealed door.

452) A 2nd life is the only hope for Heaven.

453) Heaven clearly is not here; the only hope for Heaven is a 2nd life; Christ is the only complete evidence.

454) Democrats do not fear God, and therefore have no fear of lying.

455) Believing in God without reverence for God is neither love nor trust in God.

456) Supporting abortion is not fearing God's wrath for unrepentant murder.

457) Fear rejecting God, and trust God-Christ's-Spirit.

458) Have a reverential fear of God.

459) Democrats do not revere Gods Ten Commandments.

460) Democrats do not revere life for people, because they do not revere God.

461) Democrats make a mockery of discerning Philosophers while lauding Abortionists as Philosophers.

462) Democrats do not believe in Christ's tangible Heaven nor want a neighborly Heaven on Earth.

463) Republican philosophy believes in Christ's tangible Heaven, and in sharing Heaven's peace on Earth.

464) Republican philosophy has reverence for God, and therefore reverence for life.

465) Republican philosophy has a reverence for God, and therefore reverence for truth.

466) Democrats have no respect for God, and therefore, no respect for truth.

467) Democrats have no respect for God, and therefore, no respect for life

468) Hating God is NOT a philosophy.

469) Hating God is a hate for life and reason.

470) God is the reason for reason.

471) Love reconciliation.

472) Love reconciliation's Supreme Source.

473) Love the Supreme Source of life.

474) Love the King of higher power.

475) Love the King of forgiveness who endured a crown of thorns.

476) Aspire to see a crow of gold replacing the crown of thorns.

477) The crown of thorns mocked Christ's implication of being King above all false gods.

478) Steer away from lies.

479) Steer away from scorning.

480) Spiritual child of pros not cons.

481) I am a pro not a con.

482) I am a child of life not destruction.

483) I am a child of life not deaths chains.

484) I am a child of true freedom not bondage to sin.

485) I am a child of unending hope not oppression.

486) I am a child of unending hope not hopelessness.

487) I am a child of infinite hope.

488) I am a child of resurrection power hope.

489) I believe in only living twice with Christ.

490) I believe in a second life with Christ my King.

491) I am a child of Christ's forgiveness.

492) I am a child of Christ's mercy.

493) I am a child of Christ's grace.

494) I am a child of Christ's eternal gift.

495) I am a child of Christ's love.

496) I am a child of Christ's resurrection.

497) I am a child of Christ's ascension.

498) I am a child of Christ's transfiguration.

499) I am a child of Christ's plan.

500) I am a child of Christ's eternal will.

501) Resist misconceptions.

502) Stop stereotyping Republicans.

503) Love your Republican neighbor.

504) Love your Democrat enemy of life.

505) Love bigoted People with forgiveness and truth.

506) Dead gods can't save.

507) Dead gods can't forgive.

508) Dead gods don't bring another day.

509) Outlaw Governments Baby Slaughterhouses.

510) Forgiveness does not exist without Christ's Bible.

511) Stretch your spiritual muscles.
512) Stretch your G-C-S faith muscle.

513) Christ is my excuse for every good effort.

514) My excuse for what? Being better than you?

515) We would be stuck with the Devil without repentance gift.

515) Life is a gift; gifts are for enjoyment.

516) Truth is a quest NOT a jest for vain intimidation.

517) Love your Democrat enemy of life with forgiveness and truth.

518) Wisdom is better than IQ.

519) Anyone can choose wisdom.

520) Breathe Christ's Oxygen.

521) Your natural body matters.

522) Our souls need to change; our gender is what it is.

523) Life came from Christ; believe it.

524) Life comes from Christ; believe it.

525) Life's transfiguration comes from Christ after death.

526) Life's Transformation is a daily chosen awareness of Christ's will.

527) Forgiveness is for a greater cause.

528) Murderous abortion is not proper power for government.

529) Forgiving is loving.

530) Forgiveness eliminates revenge and discerns justice or pardon.

531) Test your own motives regularly.

532) Christ redeems anyone who believes and is patient with unrepentance, but we never know when mercy ends.

533) Bigotry and stereotyping are faith's that lead to Hell.

534) True compassion is NOT supported by lies.

535) True compassion is NOT a sin.

536) We can see the Stars BUT Stars cannot see us.

537) Christianity is the Religion of reconciling peace.

538) Christianity is the Religion of love put into action by God-Christ's-Spirit.

539) Jesus is my excuse for pursuing good despite unworthiness.

540) Jesus is my excuse for pursuing good despite naysayers.

541) Jesus is my excuse for pursuing good despite Mockers.

542) Jesus is my excuse for pursuing good despite Scorners.

543) Jesus is my excuse for pursuing good despite failures.

544) Jesus is my excuse for pursuing good despite Yesterday.

545) Yesterday Is missing.

546) Yesterday is missing in action.

547) Where did Yesterday go? Move forward.

548) Stereotyping is not a good record.

549) Stereotyping is a bad record.

550) Stereotyping is NOT a fruit of the Spirit.

551) Stereotyping is NOT forgiveness.

552) Stereotyping has no faith in salvation's choice.

553) Stereotyping is NOT exercising salvation's hope.

554) Both Humans and Animals can see the Stars.

555) Measure your life by infinity not money.

556) Measure your life by infinity.

557) Democrats love Women who hate Women.

558) Democrats love Women with Male genitals.

559) Democrats prefer Women with Male genitals.

560) Democrats love Women as much as Democrats love babies.

561) Democrats only love Women with aborted babies and a hysterectomy.

562) Democrats love Mothers who kill their own babies.

563) Democrats would love to exterminate Mother's Day.

564) Democrat homicidal maniacs would love to exterminate Mother's Day 100%.

565) Democrats support the most serial killings in World History; outlaw Baby slaughterhouses.

566) Happy Mother's Day Republicans.

567) Christianity is the Religion of everlasting peace.

568) Christianity is the Religion of eternal peace.

569) Christianity is the Religion that created Human neighbors.

570) Christianity is the Religion showing one Human race from God, Adam, and Eve.

571) Christianity is the Religion with the only Living God.

572) College degrees do not make you neighborly.
573) College degrees do not make you forgiving.

575) College degrees do not make you shun stereotyping.

576) Be Non-Fiction.

577) Reach Christ beyond potential.

578) Emotional IQ + instinctive IQ vary.

579) Value other Peoples work; not just your own.

580) Without Fathers; Mothers do not exist.

581) Sanity's boredom = insanity's door.

582) Gender preservation preserves Humanity,

583) Gender destruction does not transform anything; It creates an illusion.

584) Fences keep Dogs in and Coyotes out.

586) Fences make it easier to keep children from running into the street.

587) Walls give people protection from Creatures of the night.

588) Homes are built to be lived in.

589) Love is creative.

590) Discrimination is necessary; despise is not.

591) Human Genesis was born from God.

592) True compassion does not come from self-righteousness.

593) True compassion does not come from a self-righteous dead end.

594) True compassion does not come from only living once.

595) Achieve completeness with the golden key.

596) Joyful NOT prideful.
597) Contentment NOT Pride.

598) Happy NOT proud.

599) God created politics.

600) True compassion warns about Hell.

601) True compassion points to Christ's Heaven.

602) True compassion discerns neighborly justice not vengeance.

603) True compassion believes people are equally Human from God.

604) Life is not a crime.

605) Support natural Parenting goals.

606) Support natural Marriage laws for children's sake.

607) When lies become laws then flies become our Pa's.

608) A womb is not tomb.

609) A Woman's womb is a Human child's first room.

610) We all came from Noah's Ark.

611) We all came from Noah's family after the flood.

612) Nations without God-Christ's-Spirit = Nations lacking wisdom.

613) Nations without God-Christ's-Spirit = Nations with less discernment.

614) Nations without God-Christ's-Spirit = Nations lacking conscience.

615) Nations without God-Christ's-Spirit = Nations lacking Human regard.

616) Nations without God-Christ's-Spirit = Nations without any Human equality.

617) Human rights come directly from Gods Ten Commandments.

618) Only God is Supreme.

619) Property rights > money.

620) Moral freedom > immoral freedom.

621) Immoral freedom steals.

622) Moral freedom sustains life.

623) Moral freedom protects Human life.

624) Moral freedom protects individual and business property rights.

625) Immoral freedom accepts lies.

626) Moral freedom seeks the truth.

627) Immoral freedom legislates lies.

628) Immoral freedom legislates destruction.

629) Moral freedom opposes slavery; immoral freedom supports slavery.

630) Ethnicity came from language change in Noah's descendants.

631) Ethnicity came from God changing Peoples language.

632) Ethnicity came from language.

633) Ethnicity came after the Tower of Babel.

634) Under God = under Christ's "Golden Rule."

635) Under God = Police are under God.

636) Under God = Judges are under God.

637) Under God = Courts are under God.

638) Under God = Probation Officers are under God.

639) Under God = Presidents are under God.
640) Under God = Congress is under God.

641) Under God = Supreme court is under Superior God.

642) Under God = House Of Representatives is under God.

643) Under God = Senate is under God.

644) Under God = Lawyers are acknowledged as under God.

645) Under God = humility versus pride.

646) Under God = Scientists are less than God.

647) Under God = Doctors are less than God.

648) Under God = we assess Scientist's honesty.

649) Under God = we assess truth versus lies.

650) Under God = we acknowledge lies exist.

651) Under God = we acknowledge no one is perfect.

652) Under God = we get reconciliation.

653) Under God = mercy and redemption exist by eternally defining action.

654) Under God = second chances exist.

655) Under God = we believe in second life possibilities.

656) Under God = we believe in second life evidence and potential.

657) Under God = we believe in 2nd life hope.

658) Under God = we forgive with purpose.

659) Forgiveness in justice eliminates revenge for neighborly discernment.

660) Forgiveness is ordered by God.

661) Forgiveness is a key to loving neighbors rightly.

662) Loving neighbors rightly loves Gods 10 Commands for God, Self, and Humans.

663) Love Humans with Christ.

664) Love neighbor + enemy = all neighbors = all Humans with Christ's forgiveness.

665) There is something between the lines.

666) Resist Satan.

667) Get close to God.

668) IWABW = I want a better World.

669) PPTP = Proverbial, poetic truth pursuit.

670) PPTPB = Proverbial, poetic truth pursuit book.

671) I want a better world with more of Christ.

672) IWABW with more faith in Christ.

673) TPIC = truth pursuit in Christ.

674) T-PUG = truth-pursuit under God.

675) LYN-UG = Love your neighbor - under God.

676) PTP = proverbial truth pursuit.

677) I want a better World with more faith in Christ.

678) I want a better World with more peace in discussing evidence of God.

679) I want a better World with more freedom to discuss evidence of Heaven.

680) I want a better World with more freedom to assess a living God.

681) I want a better World with more freedom to assess God's Heavenly clues.

682) I want a better World with more freedom to discuss Christ's 2nd life clues.

682) I want a better World with more forgiveness.

683) I want a better World with less revenge and more discerning justice.

684) I want a better World with less revenge and more neighborly justice.

685) I want a better World with less revenge & more due process under God.

686) I want a better World with more due process under God.

687) I want a better World with more neighborly justice under God.

688) I want a better World with more neighborly mercy under God.

689) I want a better World with more discerned justice under God.

690) I want a better World with more Human equality under God.

692) I want a better World with more resolution exercised under God.

693) I want a better World with more love for neighbor's property.

694) I want a better World with more reverence for God's love.

695) I want a better World with more reverence for Science under God.

696) I want a better World with more reverence for truth over lies.

697) I want a better World where lies against neighbors do not stand.

698) I want a better World where laws support natural Parenthood.

699) I want a better World where laws support natural parental responsibility.

700) I want a better World where marriage laws are honest and do not support government corruption.

701) I want a better World where marriage laws are natural and do not support government kidnapping.

702) I want a better World where marriage laws are real and do not

support government making children into slaves of government.

703) I want a better World where Parenthood laws are real, and help children to know their real Father and Mother.

704) I want a better World where Marriage laws are true and help children to know their real Father and Mother.

705) I want a better World where unrepentant Baby killers cannot be qualified as Doctors.

706) I want a better World where government cannot murder Babies.

707) I want a better World where government outlaws the murder of Babies.

708) I want a better World where government is expected to view Babies as Human.

709) I want a better World where government is expected to enforce against killing Babies.

710) I want a better World that values dating for the purpose of being monogamous.

711) I want a better World that values God as Redeemer versus oppressor.

712) I want a better World that values natures laws for good awareness in children.

713) I want a better World that values natures laws for protective awareness for children.

714) I want a better World that values natures laws for widespread natural parent protective instincts.

715) I want a better World that values Police being under God.

716) I want a better World that values Judges being under God.

717) I want a better World that values Courts being under God.

718) I want a better World that values government being under God.

719) I want a better World that expects government to be under God.

720) I want a better World that expects Politicians to be under God.

721) I want a better World that values Politicians being under God.

722) I want a better World that values Citizens as God's creation.

723) I want a better World that values Citizens as created in God's image.

724) I want a better World that values Citizens as neighbors with private property authority.

725) I want a better World where all authorities are valued under God.

726) I want a better World where Parents are valued under God.

727) I want a better World where enemies are assessed justly as neighbors.

728) I want a better World where enforcement protects people with Gods Ten Commandments.

729) I want a better World where addicts property is equally protected.

730) I want a better World where Gods Ten Commandments protect everyone.

731) I want a better World where Gods Ten Commandments are valued over Man's flawed preferences.

732) I want a better World where Gods Ten Commandments are valued over Man's changing priorities.

733) I want a better World where Scientists are expected to make safer medicinal alternatives to street swindling forms.

734) I want a better World where people are taught the value of medicinal regulation over unregulated.

735) I want a better World where people are taught realistically about

various medicine purposes and dangers without oppressive demonizing.

736) I want a better World where people are not imposing Illegitimate unpardonable sins on society.

737) I want a better World where medicinal dependency is properly considered as curable.

738) I want a better World where proper medicinal use is less of a stigma than thievery.

739) I want a better World where avoiding unplanned pregnancy is the goal without an abortion option.

740) I want a better World where baby killers are not allowed to call themselves "Planned Parenthood".

741) I want a better World where the only Living God rightly is the basis for defining true Religion.

742) I want a better World where more 2nd chances are offered to citizens also.

743) I want a better World where 2nd chances are universally offered.

744) I want a better World that seeks to be more like Heaven.

745) I want a better World that ponders how to be more like Christ.

746) I want a better World that ponders Christ's commands to Love.

747) I want a better World that follows Christ's commands to Love.

748) I want a better World that makes it compelling to Worship God in Spirit & Truth.

749) I want a better World compelled to do their best; thereby, recognizing need for prayer.

750) I want a better World remembering their Mortality and need for prayer.

751) I want a better World recognizing neighbor equality from Noah's Ark.

752) I want a better World recognizing neighbor equality "For all have sinned".

753) I want a better World recognizing neighbor equality because we are all born & all die.

754) I want a better World recognizing neighbor equality because we all need to manage our behavior.

755) I want a better World recognizing neighbor equality because we are one Human race from Creations God.

756) I want a better recognizing Human equality in that Women of all Ethnicity's have the same menstrual cycle system.

757) I want a better World where 1+1 still = 2.

758) I want a better World where more people sing and others know when to stop.

759) I want a better World where repentance is recognized as a privilege.

760) I want a better World where repentance is recognized as a gift.

761) I want a better World where repentance is recognized for a better path.

762) I want a better World where holy pleasure validates a good side to pleasure.

763) I want a better World where holy pleasure is recognized as beneficial.

764) I want a better World where these requests help the next generation.

765) I want a better World with real Scientist FDA advisory NOT racist Evolution's fake Scientists.

766) I want a better World with real Scientists in Hospitals NOT racist Evolution's fake Scientists.

767) I want a better World with real Scientists making medicine NOT racist Evolution's fakes swindling our streets.

768) I want a better World where real Scientists confirm truth of physical addictions only having a 3-day addiction withdrawal phase; therefore, giving hope for people to stick through 3 days of pain, and then feel the healthy sobriety feeling again.

769) I want a better World where real Scientists confirm that after physical addiction phase using a drug again is a choice not an addiction or a relapse to declare one incurable as if it is not a choice, and as if it is an unpardonable sin when using medicinally is not a sin at all.

770) Stay in Christ's "Comfort Zone."

771) My rights come from Gods 10.

772) Property rights are more valuable than money.

773) Rejecting God = rejecting wisdom.

774) Human Authority under God.

775) Christ's Politics matter most.

776) Do not wake up on the wrong side of the dead.

777) Everybody dies - Christ rose from the dead.

778) Preferring Hell is extreme insanity.

779) Change for Christ's Kingdom.

780) Love your soul more than your sin.

781) I am a Christian because I want to go to Heaven.

782) I want the best life in Christ's Heaven.

783) Eternally optimistic in Christ.
784) Christ's forgiveness would be worthless without His resurrection.

785) Christ still forgives because Christ rose from the dead.

786) No better dream than Christ's Heaven.

787) Planned mutilation is NOT planned Parenthood.

788) The Bible does NOT okay stealing from medicinal consumers.

789) Police enforcement's top priority should be Gods 10 Commandments.

790) Democrats want Gangster & Abortionist Police worse than any Police ever before.

791) Christ's Eternal life is the biggest handout in History.

792) More diversity within moral realms not immoral diversity.

793) Immoral freedom steals - moral freedom protects.

794) Only way to ignore that abortion is murder is to silence truth speech; stop letting Democrats silence truth.

795) Odd how people get angry about false racism while ignoring true racist Evolution - Republicans propose peaceful resolutions either way, such as the freedom to point out Evolution's lie.

796) False Evolution Science has bred thievery through deception.

797) Democrats oppose the death penalty for murderers while supporting the death penalty for Babies, and while supporting Christians being killed by Islam cults in other Nations, and while promoting the inviting of those same murderous cults to cross into America's borders and into all Nations borders worldwide.

798) Dignity & mutual respect come from Biblical beliefs, but Evolutionary lies of inequality disregard both dignity & mutual respect.

799) Take care of your own house & nation.

800) Democrats putting immorality into law = Tyrannical slavery.
801) The Southern Democrat flags should in fact be replaced.

802) The American flag actually indicates one race, and that Police should be under God.

803) Every American problem was always less of Christ; the solution is

more of Christ.

804) False science lies about "Sahara Desert" Whale bones from 10's of millions of years ago are easily traceable to Noah's flood.

805) Evolution will not grow wings in Hell.

806) There is no such thing as Black or White skin; all Human skin tone ranges from dark brown to light beige; meaning all Humans are a shade of brown.

807) God is NOT Colorblind; God created all colors, and He loves His whole creation.

808) We can live a better life; we can gain knowledge and solutions, but the 2nd life only comes from resurrected God.

809) Microscopes have not been around long; the Bible written by people with eyes has.

810) Use dungs Methanol for fuel, instead of ethanol from food.

811) Do not know what to pray? Pray, "Thy Kingdom Come" from the Lord's Prayer.

812) Support Schools that teach children God's laws of Nature.

813) Oppose Schools that teach Children against God's laws of nature.

814) "Under God the Creator" as defined by America's "Declaration Of Independence".

815) Reasonableness understands if you want peace - support good Police.

816) Major government corruption are Democrats pushing moral decline for the sake of government supremacy.
817) Natural Family can struggle, but natural family laws are NOT built on a lie for greedy supremacist government power.

818) Christ was predestined to die and rise again for everyone to have a clear choice.

819) Value other Peoples labor not just your own.

820) We all have more than one eye cue (IQ).

821) The peace from "peace and quiet" never lasts long without the 2nd life Christ as our only God.

822) Pull time out of the box with Christ's eternal life.

823) Give up giving up by looking up and living up.

824) All people deserve to be shown God's love. Christ showed so, said so, and commanded so.

825) All Ethnicity's, and all individuals are equally sinners who need to choose Christ's resurrection power as God's, and His forgiveness for everlasting life.

826) Allow struggles to elevate you to time alone with God-Christ's-Spirit.

827) Be a directional signal for Heaven, and be a stop sign for Hell.

828) Temperance is a highly pursued virtue on success road.

829) Honor God's gravity for without it we dissipate into oblivion.

830) Godly encouragement is an infinite bank account; monetary help is very limited.

831) Believers in Christ should actively use their infinite Godly encouragement Bank Account.

832) Lasting love does not exist without Christ & His Bible.

833) Lasting life does not exist without Christ & His Bible.

834) Lasting hope does not exist without Christ & His Bible.
835) Life does not exist without Christ & His Bible.

836) Lasting joy does not exist without Christ & His Bible.

837) Lasting peace does not exist without Christ & His Bible,

838) Lasting goodness does not exist without Christ & His Bible.

839) Lasting gentleness does not exist without Christ & His Bible.

840) Lasting faith does not exist without Christ & His Bible.

841) Lasting temperance does not exist without Christ & His Bible.

842) Lasting patience does not exist without Christ & His Bible.

843) Lasting meekness does not exist without Christ & His Bible.

844) Lasting forgiveness does not exist without Christ & His Bible.

845) Lasting mercy does not exist without Christ & His Bible.

846) Everlasting mercy is not experienced without faith in Christ as God & Lord.

847) Everlasting peace is not experienced without faith in Christ as God & Lord.

848) Everlasting life is not experienced without faith in Christ as God & Lord.

849) Everlasting joy is not experienced without faith in Christ as God & Lord.

850) Everlasting love is not experienced without faith in Christ as God & Lord.

851) Everlasting patience is not experienced without faith in Christ as God & Lord.

852) Everlasting goodness is not experienced without faith in Christ as God & Lord.

853) Everlasting gentleness is not experienced without faith in Christ as God & Lord.

854) Everlasting hope is not experienced without faith in Christ as God & Lord.

855) Everlasting forgiveness is not experienced without faith in Christ as God & Lord.

856) Everlasting redemption is not experienced without faith in Christ as God & Lord.

857) Everlasting repentance is never experienced without faith in Christ as God & Lord.

858) Everlasting temperance is never experienced without faith in Christ as God & Lord.

859) Everlasting faith is never experienced without faith in Christ as God & Lord.

860) Everlasting property protection is never experienced without faith in Christ as God & Lord.

861) Everlasting life protection is never experienced without faith in Christ as God & Lord.

862) Everlasting 10 Commandment protection is never experienced without faith in Christ as God & Lord.

863) Everlasting truth without lies is never experienced without faith in Christ as God & Lord.

864) Everlasting life with no more crying is never experienced without faith in Christ as God & Lord.

865) Everlasting life with no more pain is never experienced without faith in Christ as God & Lord.

866) Everlasting life with no more sorrow is never experienced without faith in Christ as God & Lord.

867) If a believer is not sharing Christ, and/or is not supporting venues that share Christ, then holy love is not being shared, and neighbors are not seeing rightfully commanded love from that doubtful believer.

868) Genuine Christianity is the only true Religion with evidence of the only Living God.

869) Supernatural love is not blind; It has the biggest vision in the Universe.

870) Lies hurt; truth helps.

871) Test your own motives regularly.

872) Forgiveness is the path where wisdom can walk.

873) Wash your brain with truth.

874) Wash your brain with clean water.

875) Choose Heaven not Hell.

876) Death hurts; infinite truth supersedes.

877) Dry ice hearts have no eternal blood flow.

878) Forgiveness diffuses the power of lies.

879) Invest in Heaven - the greatest investment.

880) Lies bite - reality is a flashlight.

881) Do not be a tempter of evil; Satan is a tempter of evil.

882) The "Master Poet" is the Holy Spirit.

883) God is real despite hypocrites.

884) Emotionalism is a nutty god.

885) Stereotyping positively is just as wrong as stereotyping negatively.

886) God created luck with lightning storms; go indoors & improve good luck.

887) God does not promise tomorrow.

888) Spirit fruit living redeems time.

889) God's Spirit and Truth do not come separately.

890) It seems that teaching forgiveness would have the largest following.

891) It seems that teaching redemption would have the largest following.

892) It seems that teaching eternal salvation would have the largest following.

893) It seems that teaching eternal life would have the largest following.

894) It seems that promoting property protection would have the largest following.

895) I love opening a door in Winter without a Spider in my face.

896) Good domino effects are better than bad ones. Support natural Parenthood laws.

897) Supporting natural Parent responsibility, means supporting natural Marriage laws.

898) Be different not indifferent.

899) Without gratefulness for what we have - we think we have nothing to give.

900) Democrats most dreaded day of the year = Mother's Day.

901) Some People do not think I qualify to speak, but I have studied more Bible than Moses.

902) Pride is a perverting spirit.

903) Always pursue revival not the inevitable Rapture.

904) Supernatural redeeming justice seeker.

905) Doubting Christ is deathly boring.
906) Promoting dead gods as Religion is false advertisement.

907) Recognize Democrats speech slavery methods.

908) Build a double-wide wall at Canada's border.

909) America was formed by freedom seeking Settlers who escaped Theocratic slavery.

910) Democrats goal? Lure 7 billion & Make Gov law to abort all babies?

911) Human cultures should not be used as diversions from eternal Heavenly culture.

912) Christ showed we need to share evidenced action not just words.

913) Sons of God = Sons of redeeming love.

914) Rebel against lies that reject Christ & His laws.

915) CNN is the real White Supremacist using Black racists to promote their preferred racist segregation.

916) My goals are so high - only God can see them clearly.

917) Why do so many believe in Christianity? Because, Christ is the only one in History to permanently rise from the dead.

918) Yes, I believe in a 2nd life & it gets lesser weird the more I review Christ's evidence.

919) Democrat slavery is real - Islamic Terrorists are Democrats Global supremacist crackers.

920) Democrats have always advanced the Slave Mastering murderers & thieves in society.

921) Anyone can administer death, but for a 2nd life one must rely on infinite resurrection's God.

922) Muslims from "Theocratic Nations" immigrate as Theocratic soldiers (politicians) NOT Civilians.

923) People should be able to inquire about the validity of any god without being threatened physically.

924) Follow God's truth & Spirit fruit road.

925) Republicans love USA because to them it represents defeating

slavery "under God".

926) Republicans do NOT represent slavery - Islamic & American Democrats regimes do.

927) White American Democrats are the true Crackers promoting Black baby abortion murder.

928) Pay Musicians for their performances.

929) Music is an enjoyment of Creation, why not use it for the joys of Creation's hope & the Creator & the lasting peace only He can give.

930) Aspire to be peaceful minded in that you never need to worry about life fully coming to an end in Christ.

931) If you do not have any "drama" then you are not living.

932) Be an "Infinite Journey Being".

933) Live for infinity or you will die bored & hopeless with depraved destiny.

934) I like peace, quiet, and noise.

935) Seek the "Redeeming Key".

936) Do not be a passing whim like those who could have built an Ark before the flood of Noah's time.

937) Achieve completeness with Christ.

938) Real wealth comes from revering the God over all.

939) Accepting life and death's realities is humility.

940) The mind is too vast, imperfect, and multi-faceted not to trick itself = That is one reason that we need God's good laws, not counterproductive, disorderly, and corrupt laws.

941) Property rights come from God, not from grades that test your memory.

942) Do not steal redemption from people.

943) Do not steal by over punishing.

944) Jesus is not just real in songs - He is real all the time.

945) Most Republican news is afraid to lie, because they believe that liars go to Hell.

946) Abortion supporters calling pro-lifers racist is a complete contradiction.

947) Outlaw White Abortionists from killing Black babies - Outlaw Black Abortionists from killing White babies. Make those provisions, but also outlaw all abortions, abortion clinics, and Abortionists.

948) When will White Democrats racist minds evolve beyond Evolution? They only get over Evolution via repentance.

949) White Globalism Supremacy is what White Democrat American media wants.

950) The lowest living life form on the planet by their own Evolutionary defining of themselves = The White Democrat American.

951) The White Democrat American is the true "Cracker" who promotes killing Black babies.

952) Humbly remember you are a sinner and discern your steps.

953) Quality in life comes from revering life's Creator.

954) The unreasonable Democrat Party has always been known for its mobs.

955) Do not murder your own soul.

956) Pharisees do not go to Heaven.

957) People who pretend to believe that Christ is God, don't go to Heaven.

958) People who think their goodness can get them to Heaven without trusting Christ as God, don't go to Heaven.

959) People who hate repenting to Christ, don't go to Heaven.

960) Jesus flying toward Heaven like "Superman" is plenty evidence.

961) Pro-death is a trait of Hell.

962) We are all Adamites, we are all Noahmites, we are all Humanites.

963) Blame God correctly.

964) Loving evil - desires destruction.

965) Trust people who believe in Hell to be more honest than those who do not.

966) Can you go to Hell for a medicine? Answer = If you love it more than God, Yes.

967) Can you go to Hell for a medicine? Answer = If you use medicine to harm people, Yes.

968) Can you go to Hell for a medicine? Answer = If you believe medicine is the unpardonable sin, Yes.

969) Can you go to Hell for a medicine? Answer = If you think medicine will get you to Heaven, Yes.

970) Can you go to Hell for a medicine? Answer = If a medicine overdose kills you and you did not believe in God before that, that overdose does not give you trust in Christ as God before you die, and we go to Hell if Christ is not our God.

971) The Evangelical community was formed from escaping Theocratic Government Catholic slavery.

972) If Democrats can call Republicans racist, then Republicans can call Democrats stupidly extreme racists, because they actually are + they support racist Evolution.

973) Democrats are racist Evolutionist enablers.

974) Permanently isolated on an Island - Christ's resurrection power still

truly matters.

975) Democrats have murdered millions of Black babies via abortion / Republicans murdered ZERO.

976) Root problems Globally = False Religions & Atheism. Noah's Ark saving God always = Pro-life.

977) Religion should be pro-eternal life, that is what Religion is supposed to be about, if it is not, then it is a False Religion.

978) If you are really against slavery, then stop silencing speech about evidence of a 2nd life, and value of life.

979) Reality - Democrats hate Republicans for outlawing slavery, in 1865.

980) I am glad to be on the side of freedom under God.

981) I am glad to be on the side of pro-life freedom.

982) I am glad to be on the side that opposes Government murdering babies in pregnant women.

983) Stop pretending like there is no God to blame.

984) Blame murderous hearts for abortion.

985) The American Indian migrated from Noah's Ark too.

986) Every Nation in the World needs good border security.

987) Don't retire your mind.

988) Job or no job, don't let your mind go out of business.

989) Make your mind be a vehicle of light in darkness.

990) Do not just be an "Earthling" - Trust Christ's evidenced 2nd life hope.

991) Christ is the only "Supernatural Alien" that you need to trust right now.

992) Democrats Truth phobia about discussing evidence of God & Heaven

should not be deemed offensive.

993) Democrats promote all stealing, lying, & killing in order to steal all Human rights commanded by God for the sake of Democrat leaders to attain Global Supremacy Governing power.

994) Do not continue letting the Democrats take the World back to legalizing slavery like they have killing babies and many other atrocities.

995) An Israelite adopted by an Egyptian Princess became the Husband of an Ethiopian Woman, and later delivered God's "Ten Commandments" to the World = Moses.

996) Ancient Whale bones found in the "Sahara Desert" are clear evidence of the Worldwide flood of Noah's time, yet, haters of God denied the possibility of a past flood when they found the bones.

997) Truth about lasting hope is good energy. Lies that oppose lasting hope is negative energy. Discernment that balances reality is logical. Hope exists. One must cater to hope in simply preparing for a successful tomorrow. The evidence exists.

998) Recognizing that hope caters to planning success - is plenty evidence of the Redeeming God-Christ's-Spirit.

999) Government has no business killing babies in a free nation, or it is not a fully free nation, if at all free.

1000) The Bible is not used in proper context without citing Christ as the theme.

1001) "Under God" we assess Science and Scientist's honesty for all Humanity equally created in God's image as our neighbors.

1002) Life breathes with forgiveness.

1003) Love People; compete with time.
1004) Awaken to life's renewal.

1005) Awake again in Earth's very end.

1006) We all came from Noah's Ark.

1007) 2nd chances - 2nd life; from Heavens Christ.

1008) Democrats actually hate immigrants and love impostors.

1009) Christ's haters are not sane.

1010) My haters are not sane.

1011) No one needs to die for Jesus; Jesus can take care of Himself.

1012) Live for your faith in Christ, and if there comes a point where you have to die for your faith in Christ with no escape, then continue to live and die with your faith in Christ eternally whether a peaceful natural death or not.

1013) Everyone looks different, even in the same Ethnicity, same family, and even twins look a little different from each other; so, what difference does it make if someone dates a person from another Ethnicity? It is no different than dating someone in the same ethnicity descended from another son of Noah.

1014) Police who support killing Babies should not be Police at all; the same applies to Doctors.

1015) Be neighborly beyond Earth's norms.

1016) The word "Race" in everyday life means "racing to get to the front of a line."

1017) When Christ rose from the dead - He proved His power to create Adam and Eve.

1018) When Christ rose from the dead - He proved His power to bring a worldwide flood.

1019) When Christ rose from the dead - He proved His power to open the "Red Sea" for Moses.

1020) When words reflect the need of the heart eternally, then Christ is behind the words.

1021) HTCR = How To Cure Racism

1022) PANW = Promote A Neighborly World

1023) CMM & LAYN = Christ Matters Most & Love All Your Neighbors
1024) CRWC = Cure racism with Christ

1025) TADC = The American Drug Cartel

1026) TWWID = The Whole World Is Delusional (Romans 3:23)

1027) Equally human ancestor from Noah's Ark.

1028) Equally human under God in His image.

1029) Earth time is limited.

1030) Time does not die.

1031) Don't be death's slave.

1032) Receive time eternally.

1033) Self managing liberty under God matters.

1034) Be saved from death's slavery.

1035) Bodies die but souls don't have to.

1036) Choose the Savior over death's slavery.

1037) All lives matter to Christ not to government.

1038) Under God governments are expected to care & be fair.

1039) My goals are so high only God can see them; I can't!

1040) Shirt truth with the World. tTt

1041) Science is real – Evolution is NOT!

1042) Don't work hard at working hard; work hard at diligence & value which reaps more productivity with truth & peace.

1043) Slavery is slavery; it is not simply Black or White.

1044) When a key to a door does not fit – you have to get the right key.

We only know one key that fits the door to permanent victory over death = Faith in resurrected Christ.

1045) The only evidenced key that fits the door for reconciling life after death is Jesus Christ & those are the facts.

1046) Death has never evolved.

1047) There is 0 evolution in conception & death.

1048) Most consistent facts of life = We were all born & we all face death.
1049) Love working toward feeling good not bad.

1050) Love working toward helping others feel good not bad.

1051) Love working toward pleasing God not Satan.

1052) Real Science supports Human History back to Adam & Eve.

1053) A False Prophet does not love neighbors and enemies.

1054) Forgiveness & mercy are always fair & right; safety measuring is the hard part of justice discernment.

1055) Complain when you cannot get out of a ditch yourself, otherwise don't complain.

1056) "Signing in" to Christianity is signing up with Christ not with other Christians.

1057) Gangsters are too quick to judge.

1058) The only true "Native land" origin of American Indians & all people is the "Garden of Eden".

1059) You could say that true Native origin for everyone today is Noah's Ark.

1060) I make EXCUSES to eat, because a body needs food.

1061) I prefer certified Doctors drugs not a certified thief

1062) If you hate Christ your last birthday is your last birthday; His lovers will celebrate age 1 trillion…

1063) Get cozy with Christ's fruit of the Spirit.

1064) Share God w/out sharing His name sometimes by being a peacemaker & forgiver.

1065) Give me dignity or stay away from me.

1066) Small minds all say the same thing = "You think too much!"

1067) One of mankind's greatest inventions is good old "cold cereal".

1068) Music is not the answer – tuning into the Creator of sound is.

1069) The #1 step to get along peaceably w/ a Police Officer = TRY TO!

1070) Pretending drugs are evil instead of people does not create safer drugs.

1071) The true DNA of racism reject the Creator of Human Beings who raised Christ from the dead.

1072) Black lives matter to liars, but not to truth tellers?

1073) Black lives matter to abortionists, but not to pro-lifers?

1074) Freedom from thieves is freedom from slavery – Police help folks to establish a distance from thieves.

1075) Teaching, funding & pushing "Evolution" is true systematic racism!

1076) Orange is not Black & freedom is not slavery & having Black slave masters is not freedom!

1077) If men are animals, then women are animals; correct? Christ's resurrection power validates / evidences God's Human creation power.

1078) Men & women do rule equally over animals. Animal rights would not exist without Human ruling them to.

1079) Opposing Christ as Creator is racist.

1080) Before America existed, nearly every Nation had slavery; America was among the first to outlaw slavery via Republicans!

1081) Police sirens & Uniforms are enough warning for people to behave – they don't need warning shots which are too risky anyway.

1082) People are tired of Black racists trying to murder Police & then acting like Police are guilty of murder when it backfires.

1083) The main ploy of Democrats faking White American racism is to lie to the Globalist community.

1084) If there is going to be "Global Government", then Republicans need to push for America to be the head, or partner in that government versus letting Democrats scheme to make us the tail. Meanwhile, continue arguing for "Independent Globalism".

1085) It appears Democrats lies about White racism are a ploy to try and make America the tail in a Global dependency State.

1086) White racism is not a big problem in America.

1087) Black racism is a big problem in America.

1088) Liberal media lying about White racism to create Black racism is a problem.

1089) Liberal media promoting Black racism to segregate racially is a problem.

1090) We can work hard in 1 place regularly that needs it without getting tired = On our minds.

1091) Truth is important even if it exonerates a "Whitee".

1092) America is actually racist against White people not Black.

1093) God is not a pharisee.

1094) Some White men can jump & some Black men cannot = Reality check for bigots!

1095) I am for Godly justice NOT social preference justice!

1096) "Social preference justice" is not neighborly / fair justice.

1097) Neighborly, fair, Godly justice assesses all sides thoroughly, discerningly & truthfully under God.

1098) God is a God of mercy who advocates mercy; social preference justice resists mercy.

1099) Tired of seeing Blacks killed in Police incidents? Complain to media = There are more Whites killed than Blacks & media never shows it.

1100) Salvation comes from a life jacket, but it also comes from using it.

1101) Why use a life jacket if you don't trust it? A life jacket works for anyone.

1102) Nobody has a racist bone; they have racist hearts; bones came from Adam & Eve equally; hearts make choices.

1103) God dimly and gradually turns the lights on each morning.

1104) Legalizing "Adam & Steve" supports every racist theory imaginable.

1105) "God bless us all, especially me; in Christ's name, Amen." Anything wrong with that prayer?

1106) One of my goals in life is to be strange to vanity.

1107) One of my goals in life is to be aware of & resistant to vanity.

1108) Serve God because people are not perfect leaders.

1109) The majority of best moves I ever made were staying away from troubling people.

1110) The best move I ever made was trusting God to go in His Heavenly direction.

1111) Why doesn't the World know South American slave trade History, or African slave trade History? Conspiracy against freedom loving America.

1112) Shirt the Gospel with the World.

1113) Sign the Gospel with the World.

1114) You can never have a perfect reaction routine for every negative person you run into, but you can nearly always remember to tune into God-Christ's-Spirit.

Many concepts in this chapter are simply what is derived from meditating on the fruit of the Spirit Scriptures God gave us through Paul in Galatians 5:2-23. We cannot learn as such when speed reading. Meditation / marinating in Biblical Scripture is of utmost importance helping us to gain wisdom, understanding, and clarity of God's Spirit and truth.

CHAPTER 10 = Healthy Biblical Foods - Nutrition Matters

Genesis 1:29 "And God said, behold, I have given you every herb bearing seed, which is upon the face of all the earth, and every tree, in the which is the fruit of a tree yielding seed; to you it shall be for meat."

FRUITS: Figs, Grapes, Pomegranates, Apples, Watermelons, Apricots, Raisins, and Dates

VEGETABLES: Corn, Garlic, Onions, Green Olives, Cucumbers, Cabbage, and Brussel Sprouts

LEGUMES: Lentils, Chickpeas, and Peas

FISH: Salmon, Albacore, Mackerel, Herring, Anchovy, Bass, Carp, Cod, Mullet, Crappie, Flounder, Halibut, Sardine, Trout, Tuna, Whitefish, Flounder, Perch...

MEATS: Chicken, Dove, Duck, Goose, Pheasant, Pigeon, Quail, Sparrow, and Turkey... Antelope, Buffalo, Caribou, Cow, Deer, Elk, Gazelle, Giraffe, Goat, Moose, Ox, Sheep...

INSECTS: Crickets, Grasshoppers, and Locusts

NUTS: Almonds, Cumin seed, Coriander seed, Chestnuts, Mustard seed, Watermelon seed, Sesame seed, Pine nuts

MILK: Cow milk, Goat milk, Cheese, Butter, Yogurt, Cream cheese

EGGS

GRAINS: Barley, Millet, Rye, Wheat, Quinoa, Buckwheat, Oatmeal, Brown rice...

OILS: Olive oil, Cumin seed oil, Corn oil, Aloe Vera oil

FLOUR: Corn flour, Wheat flour, Wheat Germ

INSECT REPELLENT / FRAGRANCE: Cedar wood, Cedar chips
VINEGAR
BEVERAGE: Water, Grape Juice, Wines, Milk...

SPICE: Mustard seed, Sea Salt, Cinnamon, Cumin seed, Coriander seed (Leviticus 11:20-23; Deuteronomy 14, Acts 10, Mark 2, Matthew 9:10, Mark 7:14-23)

(Numbers 11:5-9, 2 Samuel 17:28-29, Ezekiel 4:9-12, Isaiah 7:21-22, 1 Samuel 25:17-18, Numbers 13:23, 1 Timothy 5:23, Genesis 43:11, Deuteronomy 14:3-29)

WHAT IS MY PERSPECTIVE ON CLEAN AND UNCLEAN FOODS? DOES THE BIBLE SAY THAT WE CAN NOW EAT UNCLEAN FOODS SUCH AS PORK AND SHELLFISH? ANSWER:

Peter interpreted his dream in Acts chapter 10, which told him to consume unclean foods as a picture that he could mix with Gentile people, and eat with Gentile people. Peter did NOT interpret the dream so as to say that unclean foods are to be in his grocery list, but rather simply that he could dine with unbelievers is the indication I gather, and Gentiles in his dream I think represent anyone who is not of Jewish heritage, but also anyone who is an unbeliever in Christ as Lord. That does not mean that we consider unbeliever's as best friends, but as people we can do business with, go to a party with, meal with, and can share God and good times with...

Paul speaks more on food than Peter does, and Paul basically indicates that he never made unclean foods such as pork to be a part of his diet or grocery list, but says that if you are a guest at a house and they serve pork, then it is okay to pray over it, and eat it, so as to be cordial to those who are sharing with you.

WHAT DO I THINK ABOUT CLEAN AND UNCLEAN FOOD? DO I THINK IT IS A SPIRITUAL PICTURE, OR THAT CLEAN ANIMALS ARE SIMPLY HEALTHIER FOODS?

I actually think that the clean animals do have more nutritious value, and there is much scientific evidence of that, and also obvious evidence such as shellfish eating the dung and other things in the waters, and pork eating poisonous mushrooms, and not having a sweat gland...

AND I also think that the clean and unclean foods were a spiritual observance that I will not deeply observe here, but when Paul says to pray over pork to bless it for eating when a guest serves it, then I take that to mean that there is a spiritual significance still, and perhaps that spiritual significance honors what God said is healthy, and perhaps we are to educate on it scientifically also, although, the Bible does not indicate an urgency to teach people about clean and unclean foods who do not know about clean and unclean foods.

As for me, I choose the healthier foods, except when I have a sweet tooth, but when I am being served food by other people, I will accept pork when there is not another option, and I will pray over it in a silent prayer... I also count the pork as usable calories, but I do not consider pork as very nutritious, nor as a highly absorbable protein as clean meats, and I consider it as high sodium meat compared to other meats...

AND actually, I can put 1+1 together, in that I just gave you some modern real science on pork, and real science validates Biblical teaching on foods, and that is how I believe that there is physical health value to the clean foods God told us to eat, and there is also Spiritual value.

BUT Jesus talks about food in a spiritual comparison, and He indicates that the most important food is words of life, it is what comes out of the heart that defiles a person, and He eludes that we should not be highly concerned about physical food in comparison, indicating that in comparison to bad Spiritual food, physical food cannot defile us. Yes, that is my interpretation of Jesus words = My interpretation thinks Jesus is speaking in comparison, NOT that Jesus is saying that various physical foods do not have various effects, because obviously, various foods do affect the way you feel physically, and mentally. (Matthew 15:10-20)

Bible food list + Commentary from "Reality Harmonizer Bob"

CHAPTER 11 = Better World Reprise

1) I want a better World where more people will ponder and share the evidences that God is real.

2) I want a better World where people see enough truth of life principles to hunger for it over lies.

3) I want a better World where children can grow up with aspirations of having their own natural families, and can plan to have their own private property via "Ten Commandment" Human rights from God.

4) I want a better World where more people respect one another's property, and can have more peace and comfort in the enjoyment of their own property via it being protected by neighbors and Police who value Gods "Ten Commandments".

5) I want a better World where more people are taught to obey God in "loving their neighbors as themselves" in being forgiving, being redeeming, and in teaching and promoting redemption and reconciliation for people. These principles off God's love also apply to forgiveness and redemption in employment and housing opportunities. God also expects those who need redemption to be forgiving, repentant and redeeming for reconciliation with God and people.

6) I want a better World where people are allowed to speak against murderous abortion laws in media.

7) I want a better World where the government is not allowed to support the laws against nature.

8) I want a better World where the government is not allowed to help people kill babies, but rather will be a prosecutor of those who kill babies.

9) I want a better World where killing babies is not even a voting issue, but is permanently outlawed instead.

10) I want a better World where marriage is defined properly, and the law thereby supports natural parental responsibility.

11) I want a better World where people are expected to love and marry the romantic partner they are with.

12) I want a better World where more people are against deceptively destroying natural gender.

13) I want a better World where kind people are more enjoyable to spend time with in the beautiful outdoors, because people represent the type of kindness and comfort that comes from God-Christ's-Spirit.

14) I want a better World where people are conscientious about misconceptions of perspective, and can slow down and reflect that life is short, and reflect on what is infinitely valuable rather than being trapped inside a box of vanity and strife.

15) I want a better World where more people learn not to scorn others for things they cannot change, and are more kind, hopeful, helpful and patient with things that can change for the better.

16) I want a better World where more people are educated enough about good Nutrition without going to an extreme of eliminating animals God gave us for food, and where more people will be lesser superstitious about healthy foods having no value, because they recognize that God said not to be a glutton and to take care of our bodies, instead of many people thinking that good food does not matter because they take Scripture out of context which states that "a weak person thinks that it matters what food they eat"; that is talking about a person thinking that food either saves or condemns the soul, it is NOT saying that eating healthy does not matter for the body and mind, it is eluding that eating healthy does not save the soul.

17) I want a better World where more people learn to see beyond Economic values and to recognize Gods family values which actually helps the Economy more than twisted Economic values that encourage the splitting of families prematurely, when family can actually invest in farming and other businesses if they are getting along well, and that advantages everyone to have their family's backs - and starting businesses helps the public also...

18) I want a better World where more people learn to see past many misconceptions and where College and University is not used to trick people into debt when they are supposed to be climbing the financial savings and investments ladder.

19) I want a better World where more people learn to see past misconceptions and can enjoy being married young during the College years, and can aspire and look forward to seeing their own great Grandchildren someday. College is NOT supposed to be used to forbid people to marry.

20) I want a better World where more people recognize that postponing marriage is not mostly for finances, but rather the Bible teaches in 1 Corinthians 7 that people should get married if they are unable to maintain sexual purity, and it indicates that marriage is for each other to help maintain sexual purity under God. Religions are as guilty as Economists in forbidding marriage until after College, and many people are in a confused state about relationships by the end of College because they are pressed to be all about money rather than all about pleasing God and finding a mate if they need one to remain sexually pure for God. It is not for the State, the Economist, nor even a family to decide if 2 people are to marry - Marriage is decided between a man and woman as they see fit under God. HOWBEIT, family consultation matters, but if a couple knows they need marriage for sexual purity, I don't think they should let their family disrupt that decision. If they are able to control their passions, and marriage decisions are about getting finances in place, and family is involved, then it is okay to honor family's pace in that scenario is my take.

21) I want a better World where people recognize that all evidence shows that we are all neighbors as one Human race from God, Adam, and Eve, and God commands us to "love all of our neighbors as ourselves", and Christ teaches us that loving our enemies is included under "loving our Human neighbors".

22) I want a better World where everyone can learn Christ's superior principles of forgiveness which does not mean one has to pardon a debt (although, they can also), but it means that one forgives and seeks FAIR redemptive justice under God INSTEAD of vengeance, and one forgives in order to control their temper in the situation and to be sound minded and discerning and there are many advantages and aspects of forgiveness.

23) I want a better World that recognizes the most influential reason for having "One Nation Under God" = Having authorities know that they are expected to be "under God" in justice - Authorities everywhere, but particularly Court authorities "under God", Police "Under God", Presidents "Under God", Congress "Under God", Prison Keepers "Under God", Probation Officers "Under God", Military "Under God", Judges "Under God", The Supreme Court "Under God", Republican and Democrat Politicians "Under God", Reconciliation System "Under God", Homeless Shelters "Under God", Business "Under God" = "Golden Rule" expectation in Business... Free Market System "Under God", Private Property Rights "Under God"...

24) I want a better World where society recognizes that God created

medicine, and He gave us many warnings about medicine via talking about Wine and Strong drink, and those are the same types of warnings that are rightly placed on medicine bottles. Our Science community needs to make safer lower potency forms of all street medicines available instead of aiding only the swindler high potency formulas on the streets. Society needs to recognize that any medicine including caffeine is tricky and risky to use, but also was created by God and has some therapeutic use for people who are ill physically or mentally. Medicine use is NOT the unpardonable sin and is not even a sin at all when used conservatively and when helpful. Some will even argue that medicine is never needed; YES, it is more healthful if a person could go without medicine their whole life, and that includes going without caffeine, but it is DEFINITELY NOT the unpardonable sin, AND THE BIBLE DOES NOT QUALIFY STEALING FROM PEOPLE WHO USE MEDICINE. A simple solution is for more low potency forms of medicine to be legalized, for Scientist's to decrease potency and withdrawal features of current legal forms of some medicine, AND to DECREASE PREDATORY LAWS BY EXPECTING CONSUMERS TO BE RESPONSIBLE. Once things are properly legalized INSTEAD of having PREDATORY MEDICINE LAWS, then if a person misuses something in a safe low potency form and overdoses, then that is their own fault = Personal responsibility (obviously there should be age laws and other regulations, and I am against a lot of regulations elsewhere, but they are fitting in the medicine World). People will not be as pressured to use medicines WHEN there are legal forms that counter the underground street swindler forms and culture who literally bring pain to people via theft, predatory and dishonest lending plus violence or violent threats and are usually immune from being suppressed because the consumer has no voice and no rights under the current system, but abusive usage of products should decrease dramatically when people are given a voice and when the stigma of rehabilitation would be lifted by having a far better proper approach to all medicine which includes people knowing good nutrition, natural remedies and knowing what it feels like to feel good from good food and exercise.

25) I want a better World where people who impose illegal drugs in other people's presence as a weapon of intimidation and virtually threaten to set people up if they do not comply, as well as thievery, violence and lying against neighbors - are recognized as a much bigger problem by law and socially than mentally ill and physically injured people who are prone to use medicines for various pain or stress.

26) I want a better World where people are taught to recognize that true massive systematic racism comes from the lies of Evolution, which defines

people NOT as neighbors, but as unequal evolved animals.

27) I want a better World where racist Evolution is outlawed in schools, and the Basics of the Bible are taught that teach us that God commands all of us to love all of our neighbors in the only Human race which was created in the image of God.

28) I want a better World where it is recognized that all Humans of all Ethnicity's are equally above the animal Kingdom which were created to be a helper companion and a food source, but also to recognize that all Humans are equally sinners in need of choosing Christ's redemption for Heaven over Hell against Satan, and for a better Spiritual quality of life in this first life also.

29) I want a better World because the peace-loving God-Christ's-Spirit and His loving-kindness instills in us to all want something better in life, not something worse, and I personally choose to eternally want something better with God-Christ's-Spirit. It is right to expect that the laws in this World support the whole World being free to hear of Gods given choice of Heaven over Hell, and to be protected by His graceful, Human rights "Ten Commandments" that with reverence bring more of Heavens peace for believers and our Human neighbors, which includes Human enemies in this World.

CHAPTER 12 = Better World Poetry

U.S. MISSIONARY

A missionary -
A Christian with a mission,
A typical mission -
God's love will they give,
To people who are hungry
That they longer may live;

A typical mission -
Share Jesus with hungry,
A typical mission
'Tis good and true.

A typical mission -
Spreading love
To other Countries,
A typical mission,
To show God loves you.

A typical mission -
We all have seen,
A typical mission
'Tis good and true.

When we look at the ghettos,
And we look at the streets,
In a land full of prison's
Being run by Police;

A typical mission -
We seem to ignore,
In this special land
That we claim to adore.

Heaven's mission comes from Christ's reconciliation and His commands. "Love God with all your heart, soul, and mind; and love your neighbor as yourself." (Matthew 22:37)

A GREATER VISION

A greater vision for a better World
Comes from God above like His 2nd World.

A vision of growth for many soul's
To embrace its values that make life whole.

Love His commandments - His stewardship teaching,
But rest in His love, and comfort human need.

With God's neighborly politics all can rest assured,
That God's commandments are the most secured,

For feeding human bodies for touching many souls,
And working with plans that can nurture the whole -

Of large populations with many to feed,
A neighbor can live within this creed;

Which brings dignity to one another,
By revering God's vision beyond human blunder.

Trust God's commands, understand multi-purpose,
To love your neighbor with property rights purpose

That came from Christ's commands - that came from Christ's forgiveness,
On His painful cross where death He made our witness.

He purchases life with death - a price we cannot pay,
And His redeeming love - could not go out that way.

For later He defeated the sting of death in life,
And showed us He initiates new birth for every life.

His redeeming love fulfills His loving commands on Earth,
And also gives new life for trust in His second birth.

Redeeming life Christ gives, redeeming time Christ gives,
Redeeming space Christ gives, redeeming peace Christ gives -

To those who trust in Christ, and love His great commands,
Wisdom is shown to those to share amongst Earth's lands.

A greater vision for a better World
Comes from God above like His 2nd World.

DON'T YOU WANT A BETTER WORLD?

Don't you want a better World,
With God-Christ's-Spirit,

We all should want a better World
With God-Christ's-Spirit,

And we can make a better World,
With God-Christ's-Spirit,

Christ tells us to make a better World,

With His commandments,

To build a World around peace and love,
With His commandments,

We all should make a better World,
With God-Christ's-Spirit.

A World where people reconcile,
And truth is the common goal,

We all can make a better World,
Loving God and His commands,
Love human neighbors as our self,
Is His simplified demand,

But we tend to make it hard to do,
'Cause we skip right over God's truth,

In an effort to ignore the truth,
That there is more to this life,

Than the people that we pass each day,
Who all eventually die,

But the clear answer we have from God,
Is His resurrected life -

We can have a better World,
Trusting God-Christ's-Spirit,
We can have a better World,
Sharing God-Christ's-Spirit,

We can have a better World,
In solely God-Christ's-Spirit.

We can make a better World,
With God-Christ's-Spirit.

We all can have a better World,
Loving God-Christ's-Spirit.

I will have a better World,

Trusting God-Christ's-Spirit,

I will have a better World,
Trusting God-Christ's-Spirit,

I will have a better World,
Trusting God-Christ's-Spirit.

LIFE IS LIKE A PRISON

Life is like a prison,
Unless you have a renewing mind,
The kind of mind that never ends
In trusting Christ to redeem the time.

Life is like a prison,
With limited talents we possess,

But we can transform them all,
By pointing to Heaven with them all,

And live conformed to Christ's eternal crest. (Romans 12:1-2)

WISE UP

Wise up to the confessional,
And be a professional for the life that God has given.

Wise up to live life - rise up to give life for all who ever live.

Abort death's path escaping Christ's wrath -

Let all have an Earth day - let all have a birthday

Who have ever had a chance to be -

A God breathing child of love - living under Christ's smile above,

And having a free will choice like you and me -

To choose the God of Heavens quake - let all in Earth to Heaven wake,

Wise up to Christ's choice over Hell's unpleasant voice
Of creations soul's crying, "help" from you and me.

FIND YOUR WAY

Find your way to the bed,
Find your way out of bed,

Find your way from the bed,
Find your way to get bread,

Find your way to the bathroom,
Find your way to the classroom,

Find your way to the schoolyard,
Find your way to the churchyard,

Find your way to the movies,
Find your way to be groovy,

Find your way to the courtroom,
Find your way to the ballroom,
Find your way in the dark,
Find your way to a park,

Find your way to be funny,
Find your way to get money,

Find your way to learn knowledge,
Find your way out of college,
Find you a place to dwell,
Find a place besides Hell,

Find a way from the grave,
Find the way to be saved,

Find your way in this life,
Find the way for more life,

Find a way to diminish dying,
Find that Jesus was not lying.

Find your way to the ultimate destination of Heaven with resurrected Christ.

WISE EYES

Proverbs 15:33 "The fear of the Lord is the instruction of wisdom, and before honor is humility."

Be wise as the skies
With Christ's light ruling your eyes.

GOD'S WILL IS BEST

We must confess,
If we want God to bless,
So, our will can rest,
Because, God's will is best.

WITHOUT CHRIST THERE IS NO LOVE

Without forgiveness nobody lives,
Without grace there is no evidence of love,
Without death there is no justice against sin,
Without mercy there is no redemption from sin,
Without sacrifice there is no payment for sin,
Without burial there is no covering of sin,
Without resurrection there is no hope;

Without Christ we have no Spirit for abundant life,
Without Christ's hope we are like a candle that burns out,
Without faith in the Heavenly Father whom we have not seen - we cannot please God.
Without love for Christ - we are nothing of substance.

WHAT IS LIFE ALL ABOUT

What is life all about?
Is it just a crazy game?
Things just go in circles,

And hopelessness seems to remain.

What is life all about?
What is the answer here?
Searching, seeking, looking -
Answers come and disappear!

What is life all about?
Many answers come and go -
Until we know the one who gives
The answers we cannot hold.

What is life all about?
We have many years to see -
Peace and love come time to time
For all of us to see.

What is life all about?
To find the author of peace -
Jesus Christ God's Son did die
To meet our every need.

What is life all about?
This is the answer here -
For peace and love to reign supreme,
And all our questions cleared.

What is life all about?
Believe God's love on the cross,
And know that He is King.

What is life all about?
Glimpses of eternity where Jesus reigns supreme.

What is life all about?
King of Kings and Lord of Lords -
Life is here to see.

What is life all about?
Accept Jesus as God's gift of Heaven,
And all who believe will see.

SATAN'S LYING HELL SPELL

Every day, I see the sky,
And I see the floor,

I stand and wait to see
What God has in store.

Every day, I see the light,
And I see the night,

I sleep and slumber in God
Knowing that Heaven will be alright.
Every day, I see birth,
And I see death;

I stand in hope of new births
With Heavenly breaths.

Every day, I see the hope of Christ,
And I witness degradation from Hell -

I stand in truth,
And remind lost souls of Satan's lying Hell spell.

CHRIST MADE US WORTHY

I am worthy to receive great things,
I am worthy to receive God's grace,
I am worthy.

To receive His mighty gift of love,
To receive His blessing power and love,
I am worthy.

When God gave His Son to die,
That is what He had in mind,
To show that you and I -
We are worthy.

We are worthy,

Just as we are,
We are worthy.

Yes, Jesus died for you and me,
Endured the pain for all to see,
We are worthy.

We are worthy,
Worthy to die for,
Worthy - worthy of love,
We are worthy,
Worthy to be accepted,
We are worthy,
Worthy of grace,
We are worthy
Worthy to receive blessing -
We are worthy, worthy of eternal faith.

Hebrews 11:6 "But without faith it is impossible to please Him: for he that cometh to God must believe that He is, and that He is a rewarder of them that diligently seek Him."

MAKE GOD SMILE

Make God smile,
And walk with Him in every mile.

He gave us His truth and Spirit,
To love eternal life with our sins forgiven.

Make God smile when you sing to Him,
Make Him smile with soul's you lead to Him,

Make God smile when you share His forgiveness,
Make God smile when you share His redemption.

Make God smile when you forgive small things,
Make God smile when you share His grace in all things,

Make God smile when you share His Spirit,
Make God smile when you share His truth,

Make God smile when you love your neighbor,
Make God smile when you need to do labor,

Make God smile when you love your enemy,
Make God smile when you love your frenemy.

Make God smile when you commit your day to Him,
Make God smile when you give your night to Him,

Make God smile by giving your life to Him,
Make God smile by living eternal life with Him.

Trust and receive Christ's gift of everlasting life and love,
And make God smile.

REAL BEAUTY

What is beauty?
Just look backwards
Beautiful is true -

Something that overwhelms me,
When dreams come true.

What is beauty?
A dream is in the future -
A dream comes true?

Reality is now past -
Sustaining reached dreams?
Far beyond dreams.

This is real beauty -

A permanent reality,
One dream come true,
The truth of forever,
Believing Christ's Heaven is true.

ABSTRACTNESS

What is this?
A thought?

A new path of thought?

An Answer?

A solution?

What if we all follow the path
Of clear solutions and absolute fact?

Would that bring a perfect World?
Perhaps close with contentment.

Absolute facts: 1 + 1 = 2.

Attaining knowledge of a never changing fact -
Breed's awareness.

There is more knowledge and fact to piece together.

Satisfaction and sanity for a moment,
One factual solution never stops the knowledge cycle.

Wandering off the path of finding solutions,
Even after the satisfaction of finding one -

All humans do this.

One apparent absolute = Spirit realm.

SING FOR SOUL'S ETERNAL GAIN

I know God gave my heart a song,
To sing and dance and play along,

But through some doubts and fears,
I crushed some strings and created some tears.

But still today the songs remain,

For pure repentance to play the refrain.

I drown the past in His cleansing blood,
And walk with choirs the size of floods

Who sing Christ's songs that forever remain,
For many souls to Heaven gain.

REFRESHING SOUL

Small words of Heavenly poetry,
Are big words for the heart,
That seek lasting faith, hope, and love,
From the risen Christ of redemptions new start.

POEM FOR THE AGES

When a generation comes and goes away,
It is God's evidence that is here to stay.

Many nations have gone astray,
From seeing God in night and day,

And on His cross, we did forsake,
The God of mercy in every wake,

In every age we need to see
The heart of God through sovereignty.

God did not die, God did not rise,
Without your heart upon His eyes;

And in each-day He lets us see,
His great love for you and me.

In night and day with every wake,
Our hearts can see to not forsake,

The love that God has given,
When on the cross we were forgiven.

And in the wake from Calvary,
Christ arose for you and me,

To see the way in every day,
God gives us light from night to day.
And we can live forever more,
With faith in Christ as Heavens door -

Forsaking death eternally,
Because Christ's love for you and me.

In every day, and age we see,
God's graceful poem for you and me.

POETRY WITH SUPREME REASON

Poetry with "Supreme Reason",
Should last through all Seasons,

And long for the peace of all hearts.

For Christ is the "Reason",
And to Heaven it's treason,
To deny the sacrificed love of God's heart.

THE POETRY OF ETERNAL CHOICE

A destiny awaits us all,
Our birthright to choose is tall,

For peaceful places we dream,
Innately given from the eternal King of Kings.

SEEDS SHARED FOR ETERNITY

Holy love and forgiveness
Pierce through the darkness of lies and illusion,

For the soul's lost in darkness to see,

And God's forgiveness shared,
Is a seed that counts for eternity.

HELP ME, LORD

Lord, I am pressed on every side,
I need to get through to enjoy my life;

So, please get me through, get me through the storm.
When all is down, and the road is dark,
I need to get through to enjoy your light,

So, please help me through, help me through the storm.

Help me Lord, through the night,
So, I can see the light,
Help me Lord, help me, Lord - to get through the storm.

Lord, help me, please help me through the storm.

LIFE IS NOT THAT HARD

Life is not that hard,
Life is not that hard,
Life is not that hard,
No, it's not!

Life is not that hard,
Life is not that hard,
Life is not that hard,
No, it's not!

Yes, there is some pain,
Yes, there is some pain,
Yes, there is some pain,
Yes, there is!

Yes, there is some pain,
Yes, there is some pain,
But most pain can be managed,

Yes, it can!

People can make things hard,
People can make things hard,
People can make things hard,
Yes, they do!

People can make things hard,
People can make things hard,
People can make things hard,
Yes, they do!

But you can work it out,
You can work it out,
You can work it out,
Yes, you can!

You can work it out,
You can work it out,
You can work it out,
Yes, you can!

Place in God your trust,
Place in God your trust,
Place in God your trust,
Yes, you can!

Place in God your trust,
Place in God your trust,
Place in God your trust,
Yes, you can!

TURN ETERNITY'S CHAPTERS

Read another chapter,
Make another chapter,
Write another chapter,

In seeking more wisdom beyond this life,

Know the mind of humans,
Show the mind of humans,

That God can be seen,
In every aspect of this life;

Create many words that express,
How Christ fills every loneliness
That ever existed in the souls
Of those who find God's reason to be whole,

And turn another chapter,
Make another chapter,
Write another chapter,

For all to wise up,
And choose God's Spirit,
For every chapter of Heavens eternal life.

Pro-Heaven poetry is inspired by God-Christ's-Spirit who really can care and does care.

GOD HALF KILLS ME EVERY DAY

I have had a good perspective,
And confidence continues to grow,

Many traditions distract us away,
From what we truly need to know.

Those who trust in Christ and seek Him,
Know His Bible tells us to go,

Go and tell His story of salvation,

From the destiny of Hell below.

God half kills me every day,
With sleep that passes night to day,

And in that very special way,
He reminds me not to live in vain;

God half kills me every day,

With sleep that passes night to day,

And once again I'm reminded to pray,
For wisdom that I need each day;

God half kills me every day,
With sleep that passes night to day,

To pray for dying soul's each day,
That they will know Christ's Heaven to gain;
God half kills you every day,
With sleep that passes night to day,

I pray that all will see to know,
God's grace for all from Heaven to show;

God half kills us every day,
With sleep that passes night to day,

For when in mornings we awake,
To waken desire for eternity's sake;

God half kills us every day,
With sleep that passes night to day,

With hope we choose eternal faith,
In Christ who rose from full death's fate.

CHRIST IS GOD

Christ was born into this World,
And did miracles,
He healed the blind
And raised Lazarus from the dead,

He suffered and forgave us
While on the cross,
And He let us place Him down into a grave,

He died and rose up from the dead,
He later ascended up,
To show us

There's a second life in Him.
Christ is God,
Christ is God,
He came to Earth,
And showed that He is God.
GO TELL IT!

Go, tell it,
Go, tell it,
Go, tell it,

That Jesus Christ is Lord,
That Jesus Christ is Lord,
That Jesus Christ is Lord.

Trust the Lord
With all of your heart,
And lean not on yourself,
In all your ways,
Acknowledge Him,
And He will direct (make straight) your path,
(Your path - - -)

Go, tell it,
Go, tell it,
Go, tell it,

That Jesus Christ is Lord,
That Jesus Christ is Lord,
That Jesus Christ is Lord.

God so loved the World,
God so loved the World,
God so loved the World,
That Jesus died for all,
(For all - - -)

Go, tell it,
Go, tell it,
Go, tell it,

That Jesus Christ is Lord,
That Jesus Christ is Lord,

That Jesus Christ is Lord.

Speak on your faith,
In Christ as Lord,
Trust God raised Him from the dead,
So, that your soul will be saved from Hell,
And you will be saved,
(Eternally redeemed - - -)

Go, tell it,
Go, tell it,
Go, tell it,
That Jesus Christ is Lord,
That Jesus Christ is Lord,
That Jesus Christ is Lord.

(Mark 16:15-16, Matthew 28:19-20, Proverbs 3:5-6, Romans 10:9-10, John 3:16)

THE GREATEST POEM OF ALL TIME

A poem is a time for the greatest,
The greatest of all time,
Where thoughts and songs are the clearest,
And the mind in sync with Divine.

That is the time that is greatest,
Where the heart greets the Divine,
And that is the time where all souls meet,
And write the greatest poems of all time.

GOD IS LOVE POEM

A beach with a palm tree,
The Sky full of doves,
Not have as beautiful as is God's love.

Higher than the mountains,
Deeper than the seas,
Love so benevolent,
To meet your deepest need.

SUPERNATURALLY ENLIGHTENING

The smiles in life are many,
The struggles and challenges too;

Good times and hard times are simply a breeze
That challenge the absolute.

The love of God the Father,
Whose character does not change,
Is the one guiding Host,
Who drives me the most,
To enlightening in every day.

CONCLUSION:

John 3:16 = "For God so loved THE WORLD that He gave His only begotten Son that WHOSOEVER believes in Him should not perish but have everlasting life."

Colossians 1 = Christ is God.
1 John 4: 8 = "He that loves not knows not God for God is love."
REFERENCES: Christ's Bible, Wikipedia, Politico Fact, Planet MySkull

"Planet MySkull" is my name for the brain in my skull.

Any other reference is noted beside the verse it applies to in Chapter 1.

Reality Harmonizer Bob